MARK TODI

CROSS-COUNTRY HANDI

MARK TODD'S
CROSS-COUNTRY HANDBOOK

by
MARK TODD

with
Gillian Newsum

THE KENILWORTH PRESS

The Kenilworth Press Ltd
Addington
Buckingham
MK18 2JR

Photographs by Kit Houghton
Line drawings by Carole Vincer and
C. Bromley Gardner, by courtesy of
Badminton Horse Trials

British Library Cataloguing in Publication Data
A catalogue record for this book is available from
the British Library.

ISBN 1-872082-72-6 Paperback
(ISBN 0-901366-88-9 Hardback)

Designed by Sandie Boccacci
Typeset in 10/11.5 Galliard by
J & L Composition Ltd, Filey, North Yorkshire
Printed and bound in Great Britain by
Hillman Printers (Frome) Ltd

Note: Imperial and metric units have been used
throughout the text, except where metric units
are the convention.

Contents

Introduction

The cross-country is the most exciting and challenging part of any horse trials and the one at which most of our basic training is aimed. This book deals with the training and techniques involved in all aspects of cross-country riding, and therefore includes coverage of the road and tracks and the steeplechase. Together with the cross-country, the roads and tracks and the steeplechase combine to form the speed and endurance test, the centrepiece of a three-day event. The speed and endurance puts on trial a horse's fitness and stamina; his ability to gallop and jump at speed, and to maintain that speed over long distances; his level of training and obedience; his athleticism and his bravery. It also tests the rider – his strength and courage; his ability to judge pace; to conserve his horse's energy; to know where to tackle different obstacles with a particular horse; to 'read' the cross-country course and to realise how best to get his horse to complete it within the optimum time and without jumping penalties.

In theory, the ratio of influence of the three tests – dressage, speed and endurance, and show jumping – should be 3:12:1, but nowadays, because the standard of cross-country riding by the top competitors is so good, the dressage sometimes has a much greater effect on the final results. One of the aims of the cross-country course designer is to ensure that the speed and endurance test dominates the results of an event, though not to the extent that it causes undue trouble to horses and riders.

Because the three-day event evolved as a competition to test the strength, stamina and obedience of military horses, the emphasis is still on these qualities in the sport's modern form. The dressage test is designed to show that a fit, highly-tuned horse can also be trained to perform what is, in pure dressage terms, a simple test. The basic training and obedience required to produce a good dressage test is, anyway, essential if a horse is to perform well on the cross-country phase of the speed and endurance. The show jumping is intended merely to prove that, despite the rigours of the speed and endurance, the horse is fit enough to come out the following day and perform a straightforward show-jumping test.

The speed and endurance test is made up of four separate phases. Phase A, the first roads and tracks, is normally about 5km* long and has to be completed at a speed of 220m per minute, roughly the speed of a brisk trot. Then there is Phase B, the steeplechase, which, depending on the level of the competition, is over a distance of about 3000 metres and has to be negotiated at speeds of 640–690m per minute (this is slightly less than

*1km ≃ 0.62 miles;
1 mile ≃ 1.61km.

normal steeplechase racing speed). The next phase (Phase C) is another section of roads and tracks, usually between 8 and 10km in length, and, again, is completed at a speed of 220m per minute.

That makes up the bulk of the endurance part of the competition. There is then a compulsory 10-minute break before the start of the cross-country, Phase D, which varies in length and speeds required according to the level of competition. At an international event such as Badminton the speed will be 570m per minute, and the length of the course roughly 7km with about thirty obstacles.

To help us educate a horse to perform at a three-day event he can be entered in a series of one-day events designed to give him experience at this sort of competition without subjecting him to a severe endurance test at every outing. A horse can compete at only two, or perhaps three, three-day events a year, whereas he can compete in one-day events on a regular basis during the eventing season, gaining experience in competitions that are not too taxing or demanding.

A one-day event is basically a scaled-down three-day event. There are dressage, cross-country and show-jumping tests, but the endurance element is dramatically reduced as there are no roads and tracks or steeplechase. The whole competition is completed on one day, and, simply for ease of organisation, the show jumping is usually ridden before the cross-country.

There are three main levels of competition – novice, intermediate and advanced – and there are also some pre-novice events, which are useful for training young horses. The grading system allows a horse to be introduced at a basic level to the different types of cross-country obstacles that he is going to meet later on in a three-day event, and he can gradually move up to the top level (advanced) by gaining points for being placed at novice and intermediate events.

Traditionally, the ambition of most serious competitors was to compete at a three-day event of the highest level, like Badminton or Burghley, but because of the demanding nature of these competitions, the emphasis is tending to change, and some of the one-day competitions now have a much higher profile. To me, the three-day event is still the ultimate challenge. It is a unique competition because you are relying on a horse, not just on your own ability, and over the three days so much can go wrong. This is what keeps the sport on a friendly, amateur level, and I do not think that this will ever change. I have been eventing at international level for twelve years and regard myself as one of the 'senior' riders, but over those twelve years the thrill of going to a three-day event has not diminished.

CHAPTER 1

Choosing the Right Horse

Event horses come in all shapes and sizes. You only have to look at the horses competing at Badminton to see the full range, but they will all have certain basic characteristics in common: sound basic conformation, good limbs, good movement, athleticism, courage and reasonable intelligence.

Choosing a horse will depend a great deal on what you have in mind and how far you want to go in the sport. Almost any type of horse can compete at the novice one-day event level, but if you have three-day eventing, and more specifically international three-day eventing, in mind, then the right horse is more important. Eventing has become such a competitive sport these days that you really do need to start off with good material. If you are not very experienced, it is best to ask someone who knows quite a lot about eventing and who is known to have a good eye for a horse to go with you to help you make the right choice.

Before I go to look at a horse I try to envisage the perfect animal. I have never yet found such a creature, but you have to carry a picture in your mind to compare with what you see. Your first impressions are usually the best ones. Watch the horse as he comes out of his box to see if he looks like a complete package: in other words that the front end belongs to the back end and that the legs are not disproportionately long – he should look fairly compact. He should have a bold outlook, with an intelligent eye; and a good length of neck set well on to a long, sloping shoulder.

I do not think that you need to be too particular about conformation, as long as it is basically correct. Remember, you are looking for a performance horse, not a show horse. However, I do place a lot of importance on a horse having correct limbs. They are the parts of the body that are going to be taking most of the strain during the horse's competitive life. It is difficult enough keeping an event horse sound, so you do not want to start off with problems caused by bad conformation. Pay great attention to the front legs. The cannon bone should be set on straight to the knee and be of the correct length (i.e. not too long, as this can be a sign of weakness); the pastern should not be too upright; and the horse should have strong, round hooves. One thing I particularly dislike is for an event horse to be back at the knee, as this places extra strain on the tendons.

He should also have a good amount of bone, but not too much, otherwise he will be heavy and rather slow. Coming from New Zealand, where we ride a lot of Thoroughbreds, I tend to accept lighter-boned horses than do some British event riders, but I would certainly not want anything with thin, spindly legs.

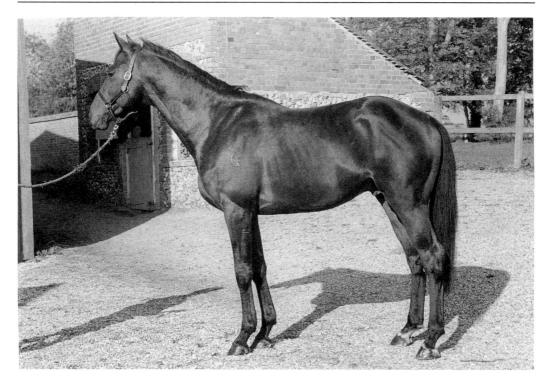

Mayhill, a Thoroughbred stallion whom I brought over from New Zealand. He looks rather light of condition in this picture, but he is basically well put together. He has a good length of rein and a back that is neither too long nor too short. He is slightly 'goose-rumped' – which means that from the point of the rump to the start of the tail his top line falls away sharply – but this can sometimes be the sign of a good jumper, as is the case with this horse. He could be deeper in the chest, but this is certainly not a big fault. My main criticism of this horse is that he is rather leggy and has quite a long cannon bone (between the knee and the fetlock), which can sometimes be a slight weakness. However, this horse is very well balanced, and otherwise his conformation is so good that I do not think it will ever cause him a problem.

I like a horse that has a good wither, one that is level with the hindquarter or slightly higher (as in Mayhill's case), as this gives you a secure feeling of having plenty of horse in front of you, and it also helps the horse to balance himself.

Splints and curbs do not bother me much as long as they are not too large or in a position that is likely to bother the horse in the future. However, you should avoid an animal that has had previous injuries such as tendon trouble, as this is likely to occur again. If you decide to buy a horse you should always have him looked at by a vet.

You may take one look at a horse and decide that he is so terrible that you definitely do not want him, but otherwise it is always worth riding him. When I first saw Charisma it was the middle of the winter in New Zealand and he still had his winter coat on. He looked like a fat, hairy pony, and I could not imagine myself and this little horse ever doing anything together. His conformation was excellent, but he needed to be about a hand higher. However, as I had driven a long way to see him I thought I might as well try him, and I then discovered that he rode like a

Alfred the Great, a fine example of 'handsome is as handsome does'. He is not full Thoroughbred, and could be described as slightly on the common side. He has a large, plain head, a very genuine expression on his face, a generous eye and big, honest ears. His neck is too short and it is set on rather low to his shoulder (although in this photograph he is carrying his head quite high). He is a little thick and heavy in the shoulder, which would account for his lack of movement for dressage, but he has a big, powerful back end which enables him to gallop well and cover the ground in the cross-country. As with a lot of horses who are not clean-bred, he tends to be a little upright in his pasterns. However, none of these faults is likely to cause him serious trouble in his eventing career.

much bigger horse. He had tremendous movement and carried himself very well, so that although he was only 15.3hh and I am 6ft 4 ins, I did not feel big on him.

I like to see the horse led up in hand before he is ridden to check that he moves correctly. When you are watching a horse trot towards you, his legs should move forward in a straight line. Many horses do swing their legs to a certain extent, which can be rather unsightly in the dressage, but I would not dismiss a horse for that reason alone. It is unlikely to affect his performance unless the swinging action is particularly marked, in which case it may put additional strain on his legs when he is galloping.

Always ask to see the horse ridden before you ride him, so that you can judge his paces and jumping ability. These days it is even more important to have a horse who moves well so that you can achieve good dressage marks, because if you are not up among the leaders after the dressage test it is very difficult to catch up after that.

You are looking for a horse who moves well in all three paces – walk, trot and canter. He should have a forward-reaching walk with a good

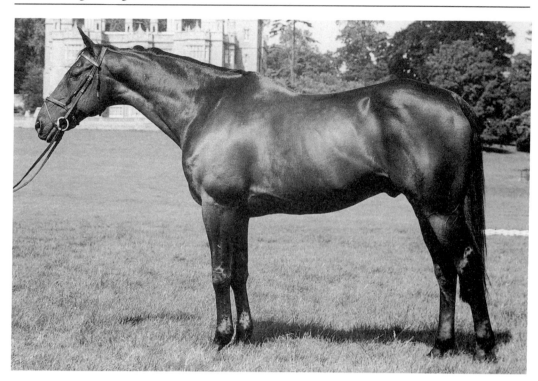

This is what I would call a lovely type of three-day eventer. One of the most appealing things about this horse, apart from the overall picture he presents, is his very handsome head. He has a wonderfully calm expression in his eye and big, honest ears. The head is well set on to the neck, and the neck is a good length and shape, which should make it easier for the horse to come into a good outline in his dressage. He has a long, deep shoulder and he is also very deep through the girth. He has good, strong limbs. The only problem with this horse is that his body is quite long, which could make him difficult to collect for the dressage. All in all, though, a lovely stamp of horse.

length of stride. His working trot need not be extravagant, but you should avoid an individual with a very short trotting stride. When you are riding the horse and you ask him to move forward in the trot he should lengthen his stride rather than go faster. To a certain extent you can improve a horse's length of stride with training, but it is much easier if the horse moves well naturally.

In trot and canter the horse should give you the feeling that he has some spring in his stride. Avoid horses who have a natural four-beat canter, as this can be very difficult to alter. The horse should have a round stride at the canter and be reasonably well balanced. Again, training can improve things a great deal, but it helps to start off with a horse that is naturally balanced.

Another thing to watch when you are riding the horse is the way he accepts the bit. Try to avoid a horse who leans on your hands and crosses his jaw. His head carriage will depend to some extent on how well he has been trained, but some horses naturally carry their heads very low because their necks are set on to their shoulders at a lower angle. This can prove

This horse creates quite a nice overall picture. He has a slightly Roman nose, which is accentuated by his white face, but this is certainly no reason to reject him. His neck and body are quite good, but he is rather long and weak in his pasterns. In this photograph he is standing well over his front leg, but many people in New Zealand would maintain that a horse who stands thus never has leg problems. He is quite long in the cannon bone, which may give rise to leg trouble, but he appears to have well-shaped feet and good hind legs. He is not as attractive as the horse opposite.

difficult later on when you need the horse to elevate himself sufficiently for the higher levels of dressage. Horses who carry their heads very high, or whose necks are set on high to the shoulder, tend to look a bit peacocky in their dressage. However, the way a horse carries his head does not necessarily relate to the way he jumps, and is not an indication of whether he will be a good or bad jumper.

It is obviously difficult to assess how well a horse jumps unless he has been broken in and has done some schooling over fences. For this reason I generally prefer to buy five- or six-year-olds. If you buy an unbroken horse you take the risk that he will not be good at jumping, but the big advantage is that you are starting with a clean slate and you can train the horse right from the beginning. Then, if things do go wrong, you have only yourself to blame.

You can gain a good idea of a horse's technique over fences by watching someone else ride him. He should lift his forearm and tuck up his lower leg neatly; and he should jump with a round back, making a good shape over the fence. However, you can get a totally different feel of a horse's ability when you ride him yourself. Ideally he should feel light and athletic,

A pleasant-looking horse, with a nice head and good outlook. The overall impression given, however, is that this horse's back end does not match his front end. He has quite a good neck, shoulder and front leg, but the hindquarter looks as if it comes from a smaller horse, and it may not be strong enough. However, without trying the horse you can never really tell; he may ride perfectly well.

so that when you take off for a fence he gives you a sensation of pinging off the ground underneath you. He should land lightly on the ground, not with a heavy thud.

When I am trying a horse over fences I like to start by trotting him into a low fence and leaving him completely alone to see how well he looks after himself. Then I gradually build up the size of the fence, but still leave the jumping to him. If the horse makes a mistake, I ask him to jump the fence again in exactly the same way to see if he learns quickly from his error. If he knocks down the same fence three or four times in a row then he is likely to be a fairly careless horse, and you have little chance of making him a great deal better.

A horse who is basically calm on the flat but who becomes a little excitable and rushes at his fences will probably learn to jump in a more relaxed manner with correct training. However, if the horse is very excitable and fizzy all the time, he is unlikely to change much, even with schooling.

There is no set rule as to whether a small horse or a big horse is better for eventing, but when it comes to personal preference, I do not like great big horses. The ideal size for me is around 16.2hh. Larger horses tend to have more trouble with their limbs, and are more likely to have wind

This is a horse that, on looks alone, I would reject. I place a lot of emphasis on the look a horse gives. This one's head is far too small for the rest of his body, and although he appears to have quite a good eye, it has a rather leery look about it. If you compare this horse's looks with the very honest expression on the horse on page 12, you will immediately see the difference. His basic conformation is satisfactory, and I may well be doing this horse an injustice in rejecting him outright.

problems. I also find that they can be slightly less athletic, although this is by no means always the case.

The size of horse that you choose will depend largely on your own physique. I feel slightly more comfortable and look better on a big horse, but if, for example, you are a small, lightly-built girl it would be ridiculous to buy a 17hh Thoroughbred as you would be unlikely to have the strength to manage him. Look for a horse who fits your physique and your ability.

If you are very inexperienced I would suggest buying a horse who already knows his job. An inexperienced horse coupled with a novice rider can lead to a lot of problems. It can be a good idea to find an older horse who may not be top level but who will be able to give you a vast amount of experience. With these older horses it is better to buy one that is very good at cross-country even if he has limitations in the dressage and show jumping, because it is on the cross-country phase that you need the most experience and help from the horse.

Obviously there are limits as to what anyone can spend on a horse, but it can sometimes be cheaper in the long run to invest in buying a better sort of horse.

The breed of horse that you choose will be partly governed by your own preferences. I like Thoroughbreds, or something very near Thoroughbred (certainly no less than threequarter bred), because they find it much easier than warmblood horses to keep up a gallop over a long distance and to maintain the fast speeds needed at top-level competitions. They are bred to go fast, so they tend to have fewer leg problems.

No horse is perfect, but the one thing I will never compromise on is an animal's temperament. I would much rather have a horse that has slightly less ability but tries for you than one that has all the ability in the world but never uses it to the full. The honest plodder, with a good, level temperament will often turn out best, as long as he has enough ability to cope with the job.

CHAPTER 2

Training

Training your horse on the flat and over jumps is an essential part of his general education; but it also makes a significant contribution to your horse's fitness when preparing for an eventing campaign. When you train a young horse you are not only teaching him to become more obedient, more supple and therefore an easier ride, but also starting to build up the muscles that he will need to use to an even greater extent when he reaches higher levels of competition.

Flat work

General training on the flat will improve the way your horse goes in both the show jumping and the cross-country, as well as in his dressage. Cross-country courses are becoming more and more technical, so it is even more important to have an obedient horse. You want your horse to come back to you when you ask him to, and to move forward when you ask him to. When tackling combination fences, particularly angled ones, you want him to stay straight. You should achieve this right from the beginning in the general flat work, where you teach the horse to go forward from the leg, to come back when asked and to remain straight.

The rider's position has a great deal of influence. You cannot expect your horse to go correctly if you are not sitting and riding correctly. The most important thing is to be able to keep the horse between your lower legs. If you grip tightly with your knee, your lower leg will come away from the side of the horse. Try to stay relaxed, then you will be able to maintain contact. To help retain the position of your lower leg, you should keep the stirrup on the ball of your foot and your weight down in the heel. Rotate your hips forward to help keep your back straight. Your upper body should be in a vertical position for your flat work, with your shoulders well back. Try to keep your shoulders and elbows relaxed, with your wrists slightly rounded, thumbs on top, so that you have an elastic feel right through to the horse's mouth. Any stiffness in your body will transfer itself to the horse and affect the way he goes.

Lungeing without stirrups and reins can be a good way of helping a rider to improve his or her balance and to develop an independent, deep seat. Generally, however, I do very little lungeing with my horses. I tend to buy horses that are already broken-in and have done some jumping, so, unless there is a special problem, I do not lunge them.

If I am having difficulty teaching a horse to carry himself in a good outline I might lunge him in a Chambon, a device which puts pressure on the horse's poll when he raises his head too high but which becomes ineffective the moment he lowers his head and neck. It consists of a strap which is attached to the girth and which passes between the horse's front legs and divides at the chest. The two branches pass through rings at either end of a padded headpiece and are then connected to the bit. Used over a period of time, the device encourages the horse to improve his head carriage. Alternatively, you can use side reins that are just short enough to maintain a steady contact with the horse's mouth.

Lungeing can help to improve a horse's rhythm and balance, but if it is not done properly it is a waste of time. A young, unbroken horse will need some lungeing, but otherwise you are unlikely to have to do much, unless you find it a useful way of calming down your horse before you ride him. Some people like to lunge their horses at a competition to allow the latter to let off steam before they are ridden. Psychologically it is probably better to let the horse have a fight on the lunge rather than with his rider.

The horse pictured below is working in a novice outline, but for my liking his poll is being carried too low. In this and the next picture my lower leg is in the correct position.

When you start training a young horse it is important to establish your priorities. You must know what you are aiming to achieve and how you are going to set about it. The most important thing is for the horse to go forward from the leg and to accept a contact with the hands. You want him to establish a rhythm and to become more supple and obedient. Then you can start to work for a better outline and more impulsion. Never try to force a horse to keep his head down and stay round by lowering your hands and pulling his head into position. You should teach the horse to carry himself in a correct outline; he should not rely on his rider to do it for him.

The learning process is a slow and gradual one. Horses do not think very logically; they learn by a process of repetition, correction and reward, so you need to make it clear to them when you are asking them to do something, and correct any mistakes immediately (though not roughly).

I have pushed the horse up into my hands, using my seat and lower leg, and as a result he is carrying his poll higher. He could now stretch his neck a little longer.

Putting the hands forward and down to encourage the horse to stretch his neck, lengthen his outline and take the contact forward. (Note that my heel has come up. If you do not have your weight down in your heel your lower leg cannot be used correctly on the horse.)

You must make sure your horse goes correctly right from the beginning and you should not accept anything that is incorrect.

Once you have the horse going forward and accepting your hands he must learn to move away from the leg. This is best done on a circle. Your aim is to hold the horse between inside leg and outside hand – in other words, you are pushing the horse away from the inside leg into your outside hand. The inside rein simply creates the amount of bend you want, and if your horse is truly between inside leg and outside hand it should be possible to give away the inside rein without the horse altering the position of his head. Achieving this is the basis of all your flat work, and it is essential for jumping.

A lot of people try to create the bend by crossing their inside hand over the wither, but if you do this it will not get you very far. It may not matter so much at a lower level, but when you come to ask the horse to do more advanced movements you will find yourself in trouble because the horse will not have learned to move away from the leg.

You can begin to teach a horse simple movements and obedience exercises quite early on. Start off at the walk, and gradually work up to doing them in trot, and eventually in canter. Transitions, leg-yielding, half halts and shoulder-in are all good exercises to make the horse more soft and compliant, and then you can move on to quarters-in and eventually to half-pass. Initially, all the work should be done in a fairly long outline, but always keep the horse active and in a steady rhythm.

When you first start to canter, do not try to make the horse go too slowly. Let him find his own rhythm and balance, particularly if you have a

Left shoulder-in. Here the horse is clearly showing work on three tracks. The near fore is on one track, the off fore and near hind are on the second track, and the off hind is on the third track. The horse is bent to the left around the rider's inside leg.

young horse who tends to be on the forehand. If you try to slow a horse too much early on, he will learn to lean on your hands. Ride forward within the horse's rhythm and when you want to slow him down, sit up, open your shoulders and just hold – do not pull back. Try slowing the canter for a few strides and then allow the horse to go forward again.

Many horses tend to canter with their quarters turned slightly to the inside. The best way to straighten the body is to think of riding shoulder-in. In this way you bring the forehand in line with the quarters, which is preferable to pushing the quarters out to be in line with the forehand. By moving the forehand you are correcting the horse within the established

Right shoulder-in. This picture shows how you can bring your inside hand away from the wither to encourage the horse to bring his forehand off the track. By opening your hand you avoid creating a false bend with the inside hand. (Note that the opening hand is still in the correct upright position, maintaining a straight line from the elbow through to the horse's mouth.)

process of training: the way to keep a horse on a straight line is to ride the horse between the inside leg and the outside hand. If you try to push the quarters over you are not riding within that basic principle, because your inside leg has to come back behind the girth to push the horse over. You must first make the horse's body straight by putting him slightly into the shoulder-in position, then once the horse is established in that position it is easy to straighten the neck.

Straightness in all paces is very important, and you simply cannot ride a horse in a straight line unless you have him correctly between your inside leg and outside hand. You must establish this from the outset if you are going to have adequate control over your horse in all his work.

Make sure that you do not overdo the schooling to start with. A young horse will not be very strong, and if he becomes stiff and sore he will not enjoy his work. Fifteen or twenty minutes will probably be enough for one session, and once the horse's muscles become accustomed to the work, the schooling period can be increased to about thirty minutes. Always work evenly on both reins. If your horse is stiff on one side you will have to

Canter work. In this picture I am keeping a contact with the horse to help him keep his balance, but I am not restricting his stride.

work a little harder on that rein, but not for any longer.

Another reason why I do not like to school young horses for long periods is that their attention span is quite short and they can become bored very easily. It is best to keep their training work to no more than half an hour, and to vary it as much as possible. You can do a lot of basic schooling while you are out hacking. For example, you can make the horse stay straight, practise a little leg-yielding, or try to increase and decrease the pace. It all helps to improve the way your horse goes.

In principle I am against the use of gadgets and artificial aids when training on the flat, but, as with lungeing when I sometimes use the Chambon, occasionally I resort to the use of running reins if I am having a serious problem in keeping a horse under control or keeping his head

The walk is very important. Here my hands are forward to encourage the horse to walk forward and take the bit.

down. However, this is a very temporary measure. I would use them for only two or three days in a row and then take them off.

If running reins are not used correctly they can create more problems for the horse and rider. The only reason for fitting a running rein is to help bring the horse's head down. Once the horse's head is in the correct position there should be no contact with the running rein. You must therefore make sure that the length of the running rein is adjusted correctly. If you ride a horse solely on the running reins and not correctly from the leg and hand then he will learn to lean on the running reins, and as soon as you take them off the horse's head will go straight back up again.

Jumping

The rider's position is as important when jumping as it is when riding on the flat. Although the basic position is similar, you have to make certain changes, the first and most obvious being that you need to shorten your stirrups. From my dressage length I normally go up four or five holes for the jumping position. However, I have very long legs; people with shorter legs may not need to adjust their leathers so much. The leathers should be short enough to enable you to bring your seat out of the saddle, but not so short that they make it difficult to keep a secure contact with your leg and seat. The upper body needs to be inclined slightly forward from the vertical position that you had in the flat work; your reins will be a little shorter, though your hands will remain in the same position. Your lower leg will probably move slightly further forward, but your weight should remain down in your heel, with the stirrup on the ball of your foot. At all times your lower leg should have contact with the horse.

When it comes to jumping, a lot of people forget all about dressage and let their flat work go right out of the window. But one of the main reasons for training horses on the flat is to make them more supple and obedient for jumping, and what your horse has learned through schooling on the flat will be put to good use when training over fences. You want him to be as calm and relaxed as possible about the whole thing. He should not think that jumping is something to get revved up and excited about. Obviously you want the horse to be keen and enjoy his jumping, but he must stay relaxed so that he can listen to what you are asking him to do.

It can sometimes be a good idea to work your horse on the flat in an area where there are jumps around, so he learns that he is not necessarily going to start jumping every time he sees a fence.

The most important thing is to teach your horse to approach his fences and to jump them without changing his rhythm. When I introduce a young horse to jumping I like to start off with just a single pole on the ground and I teach the horse to work over the pole keeping a rhythm and a good outline. That way he learns not to get excited about the idea of crossing over a pole. You want to show the horse that jumping is no big deal. Even though you are schooling over a single pole, the horse will relate these lessons to jumping small obstacles later on. Once we have progressed to tackling small fences I still like to have single poles dotted around the area where I am jumping so that I can work in and out of the jumps and just trot over the poles at random. This helps to calm the horse and reminds him to be obedient.

Once the horse is going quietly over a single pole, a line of trotting poles can be set up so that the horse learns to look what he is doing, to stretch his head and neck down and to hold an outline over a fence. Trotting poles are usually set out at distances of 3ft 6ins – 4ft 6ins (106–137cm). You can use the shorter distances when the horse is approaching in a slow rhythm and is learning to steady and balance himself. This is particularly useful for helping a very long-striding horse to learn how to shorten his stride. With the poles set out at the longer distances you can encourage the horse to lengthen his stride, which is a good exercise for a short-striding horse.

Another useful exercise with trotting poles is to space them wide apart, say 20–30ft (6–9m), and vary the speed at which you come into each pole. For example, you could trot in to the first pole on a very open stride, and then, once the horse has negotiated the pole, you could check him back so that he trots very slowly over the second pole. This teaches the horse to listen to the rider and to be obedient when coming into his fences; he learns to increase or decrease the pace into the pole and to jump the fence at whatever speed the rider dictates.

If your horse becomes a little keen or strong over the poles, you should maintain whatever contact is necessary to make him keep to a steady rhythm. Do not automatically throw your hands away to let the horse stretch down if he is rushing. Although we want the horse to stay low and relaxed over the fences, if he is running off you should keep the contact and make him wait for the poles. Sometimes the hardest thing to do is to make yourself wait, but it is a very good lesson to practise at this stage. The horse will gradually understand that he can easily trot or canter over a pole on the ground without changing his rhythm. If he trips over a pole occasionally, do not worry. He cannot hurt himself and he will soon learn to pick up his feet. As long as the horse is not rushing at the poles, let your hands go forward slightly so that he can stretch his neck down and learn to keep himself in balance.

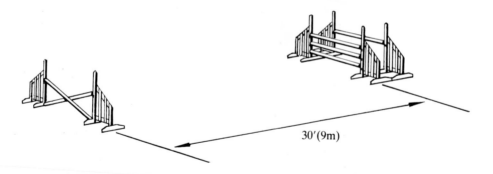

30'(9m)

I use this simple exercise to help a horse balance himself and make a better shape over a fence. Approach in trot and jump the cross-rail, then leave the horse to balance himself to the oxer. If he rushes, you will have to keep a contact until he learns to keep at a regular pace. As the oxer gets higher and wider, the horse will have to shorten himself and use himself more to clear the jump. Do not hold him off the front rail – let him learn from his own mistakes.

After this you can introduce simple jumping grids for the horse. By jumping obstacles at set distances he learns to look at what he is doing, to adjust his stride and to stay round over a fence. Start off with just one pole on the ground, 9ft (2.7m) away from a cross pole, then gradually build up with more poles and jumps (see diagram opposite). As the horse becomes accustomed to the exercise, you can reduce the distance between the jumps so that he learns to shorten himself and to become a bit rounder over his fences.

All show-jumping distances are based on a stride length of 12ft (3.6m) so when you are schooling a horse for jumping you need to keep this in mind. Your horse's natural length of stride will determine the pace at which you must work in order to achieve an average 12ft (3.6m) stride. If you have an exceptionally short-striding horse, his canter work for jumping will need to be performed in a relatively fast rhythm so that you encourage him to open up and establish the desired stride length.

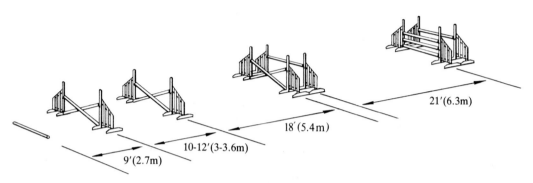

A simple trot grid: a pole on the ground to a cross-rail, a bounce to another cross-rail, one stride to an oxer with a cross-rail in front, then one stride to an oxer. Start with just the pole and the first cross-rail, and gradually add the rest as the horse gains confidence. These distances are fairly short to make the horse quicker with his front end and rounder in his jump.

Combinations or related distances in show jumping are therefore also based on a 12ft (3.6m) stride. For example, the two fences making up a one-stride double will, theoretically, be 24ft (7.2m) apart, allowing 6ft (1.8m) for landing, 6ft (1.8m) for take-off, and 12ft (3.6m) for a stride in between the fences. Within this basic framework the course designer may reduce or lengthen the distances slightly to test the horse and rider, so once you have established your horse's rhythm for a 12ft (3.6m) stride you will need to do exercises to teach him to lengthen and shorten his stride so that he can adapt to different distances. There are endless ways of setting up fences and jumping them to teach your horse to become more obedient and athletic. He must learn to jump fences at angles, to shorten and lengthen his stride, to jump off a turn, and so on. The same exercises are also good for the rider.

Many people say to me that they cannot see a stride to a fence. The best way to teach yourself is to practise over very small fences so that if you make a mistake it does not matter. Get the horse established in a rhythm, then approach the fence within that rhythm. Do not change the pace, but sit still and wait for the fence to come to you. More often than not the striding will be right, but if you do have to adjust the horse's stride, always, when schooling over low fences, go for a shorter stride rather than pushing for a long one. Then the horse will learn to shorten and round

| 6 | 5 | 4 |

| 11 | 10 | 9 |

This sequence shows a straightforward, gymnastic grid. There is a trotting pole 9ft (2.7m) from a cross-rail, then a 12ft (3.6m) bounce to another cross-rail, then 18–20ft (5.4–6m) (one stride) to an oxer and then 34ft (10.2m) (two strides) to an upright. The trotting pole at the start helps to set the horse up at the correct distance for the first cross-rail, and after that he canters on through the grid. The bounce helps to make the horse balanced and encourages him to look where he is going – he has to be quite quick and athletic to jump it. The remainder of the distances are set so that you should not need to push or hold for the fences, and the horse should be able to go through in a balanced, even manner to jump the oxer and the upright. The oxer encourages the horse to jump carefully, in a round shape, and then he should take two level strides and balance himself to jump the upright at the end.

When riding a combination like this it is important to make a good approach. The horse should come in relaxed and balanced, between your hand and leg so that you can keep him straight.

1. *The horse has stepped over the trotting pole and is looking at the fence to work out what he has to do. The rider's eye should stay in a straight line down the grid to help keep the horse straight. I like to let a horse go through on a fairly loose rein, providing he is not rushing, so that he learns to balance and help himself at the jumps.*
2. *The horse has made a nice jump over the first cross-rail.*

3   2   1

8   7

3. *The horse has the freedom of his head to balance himself. My upper body has stayed back a little to help keep the weight off his forehand.*

4. *The horse is landing neatly over the second cross-rail and is looking ahead to the oxer.*

5. *This horse is very neat with his front end: he has brought his forearm well up and his lower leg is tucked tightly underneath. A bad habit of mine is to let my body go a little to the right, which I have done in this picture. This can affect the horse's balance over a fence if it is done to an extreme. I should be looking straight ahead, with my weight central over the horse.*

6. *The horse has made a good shape over the oxer and has the freedom to use his head and neck.*

7. *I am sitting up as the horse lands in preparation to help him balance for two strides before the upright.*

8. *The horse has his eye fixed on the last fence. I have a light contact to help balance and steady him.*

9. *The horse's hocks are coming well under him as he prepares to take off. I am in a position in which my body is least likely to interfere with his forehand as it comes off the ground.*

10–11. *Again the horse has made a good shape over the upright and because he has made a rather extravagant jump with his back end, I am in a fairly upright position on landing.*

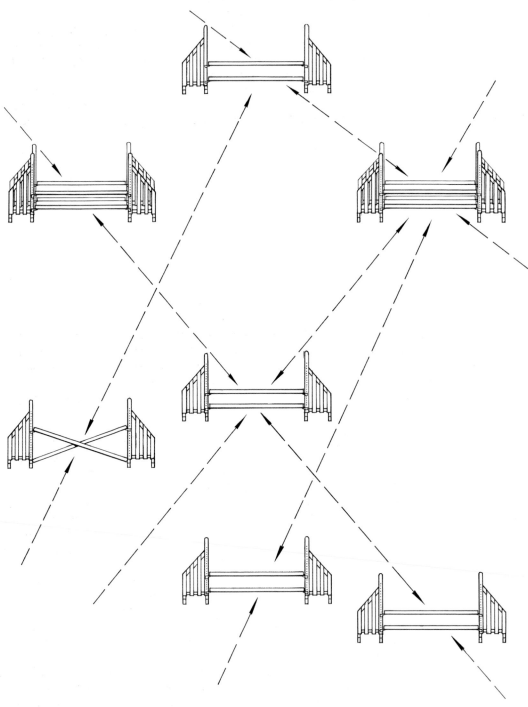

When you set up your line of fences be aware that you can incorporate angled combinations as well. This diagram shows that it is possible to create many different opportunities.

himself over a fence. If you encourage him to jump off a long stride he will learn to quicken in the air and to jump a little flat.

The worst thing that you can do when approaching a fence is to pull your horse up and make him bounce on the spot while you look for a stride, and then, when you see it, launch the horse at the fence. *Keep the rhythm.* This is the key to both show jumping and cross-country riding. If you continue working on keeping a level rhythm into a low fence, your eye will gradually start to see a stride automatically. It is possible for those without what we call a natural eye, to train themselves to see a stride.

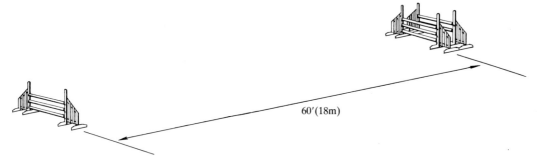

60' (18m)

These two fences, which can be jumped from either direction, are set out with a four-stride related distance, which you can use to train yourself and your horse to keep a level stride between two fences. You can vary the exercise by adding or taking out strides, and, as you become more competent, you can increase the distance between the two fences to make a normal five-, six- or seven-stride distance. This exercise will be a great help in teaching you to keep a rhythm and to develop an 'eye' for a stride.

Another good exercise to help both horses and riders – and remember that you are trying to train the horse to use his eye as well – is to set up two fences, for example, an oxer and an upright, at a distance of 60ft (18m) (four strides). You set your rhythm at your 12ft (3.6m) canter stride and approach the fence in that rhythm. The horse should jump the first fence and then stay in his regular rhythm, taking four strides before jumping the second. He should then canter away from the fence still in that rhythm.

Once you have learned to do this exercise well, you can vary the problem by taking either five strides within the same distance or, when the horse is very experienced, only three strides. To do the five strides you will need to come in on a slightly slower rhythm, jump the first fence and then hold the horse to take five level strides before jumping the second fence. This way you are teaching yourself and the horse to adjust the length of stride, and you will gradually get a feel for the horse's different lengths of stride.

You must learn to be aware of factors that will affect the length of stride that you need to ask for. For example, if you are aiming to take five strides between the two fences and you jump the first fence off a rather long stride, it will make the distance between the two fences even shorter, so you will have to be a little stronger and more determined to sit up and wait

| 6 | 5 | 4 |

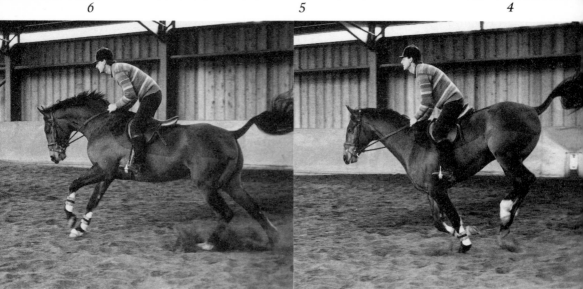

| 10 | 9 |

Cantering to a single fence.

1. *The horse is balanced and looking to the fence. My weight is down in the heel and my seat is in contact with the saddle, balancing but not restricting the horse.*
2. *My hand follows the horse to the fence and the horse starts to set himself up for the jump.*
3–4. *The horse lowers himself further, balancing himself in preparation. (Note that throughout these four pictures my position has not changed. I have tried to stay in balance with the horse so that he in turn can balance himself to give the best jump.)*
5. *On take-off I keep the same contact as I had on the approach. Again, I have tried to stay in balance without throwing my weight forward, so that I do not interfere with the horse as he lifts his forehand.*

3   2   1

8   7

6. *The angle of my hip closes at the highest point of the fence. Ideally, I would like to see the horse lift his forearm higher. Some horses just do not or cannot jump that way, and I have found it virtually impossible to change a horse's jumping technique to any great degree. However, this horse does achieve plenty of height to compensate.*

7. *My upper body starts to come up in preparation for the landing.*

8. *The horse finishes the jump well.*

9. *On landing we are back in balance. My weight is down in my heel, my head is up and I am looking forward.*

10. *I am now in a position to ride away from the fence in a controlled and balanced manner.*

for the five strides. When you are doing the same istance on four strides, if you meet the first fence a little slow and deep you then may have to allow the horse to lengthen his stride slightly to meet the second fence at the correct place.

You can construct these two fences any number of strides apart (four, five or six), and within that distance you can add or take away strides. The important thing is that you learn to control the length of the horse's stride and keep a rhythm on approach, in between and after the fences.

Once you and your horse are riding this exercise correctly and confidently you can start to work on related distances with more than two fences, and then perhaps vary the distances by a few feet. For example, you could make the strides slightly long, at 63ft (18.9m), so that you have to ride forward for the four strides; and then allow only 45ft (13.5m) for the three strides, which will ride a little short, so that you then have to shorten. In show jumping and in cross-country the distances will not always be set out perfectly. The fences will often be constructed in such a way as to create tests of the rider's control, so it is very important that you are able to lengthen and shorten your horse's stride to fit the distances.

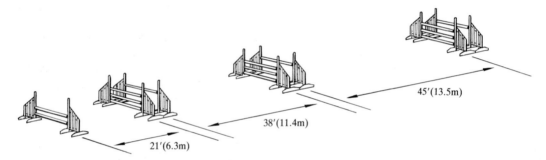

A basic canter grid with some altered distances. Approach the first fence, which should be only about 2ft (60cm) high, in a steady canter. The first stride is short. The second distance is a little long for two strides so you will have to move the horse forward to the third fence. The 45ft (13.5m) distance is short for three strides, so you will then have to steady the horse for the last jump. This is a good exercise to teach a horse to lengthen and shorten within a line of fences. The number of strides and the distances can be altered to create numerous variations, and the grid can be jumped from either direction, providing each element has a groundline on both sides.

You can go on to increase the complexity of the exercises by constructing a canter grid with four fences. There could be 21ft (6.3m) between the first and second elements (i.e. one short stride), 38ft (11.4m) to the third (two longer strides), and 45ft (13.5m) to the fourth (three shorter strides). As the horse jumps the first fence he will have to shorten to the second. When he lands over that he will have to move forward to make the two strides to the third, and then he will have to shorten again to fit in the three strides before the last (see diagram above).

This is an ideal exercise for the rider to practise the different hand releases. There are two basic releases: the short release, when the hands go from their normal position to about six inches (15cm) up the horse's neck;

and the long release, when the hands go about half way up the horse's neck to allow him complete freedom of his head and neck over a fence. The short release helps to constrain the stride and the jump, and keeps the horse short and round over his fence; and the long release encourages him to stretch out over a fence and keep moving forward on a long stride, also allowing him complete freedom over the jump.

Once the horse is jumping confidently through small grids, I like to go back to single fences to make sure that he is keeping his rhythm over a small obstacle. Whatever gait you are in, the horse should maintain the same speed into the fence; he should then jump the fence and maintain the same speed away from it. I do not like horses who rush into their fences and then tear away from them. This problem is usually caused by riders getting over-anxious on the approach to a fence and firing the horse at the obstacle. If you can make yourself sit still coming into the fence, and wait for the horse to jump it, then you very seldom end up with a rushing problem.

If the horse tends to rush off after landing from a fence or a grid, do not immediately grab at his mouth and pull him up, otherwise he will think that he is going to be grabbed in the mouth every time he reaches the end of the grid and this will make him worried. Let him take a few strides, then sit up and slowly bring him back to the pace at which you want to go. If necessary, circle him to bring him back, and then once you have him under control and balanced again, come back to trot or walk. It is a good idea to ride some simple exercises on the flat, such as shoulder-in or lengthening and shortening of stride, before you approach another fence or grid, so that the horse learns to pay attention and be more obedient.

Always aim for the centre of the fence. If your horse tends to drift to one side, use the opposite hand with an open rein to encourage him to move back to the centre. Using cross poles gives the horse something to aim at, and he will normally go for the lowest point. There are several ways in which poles can be used to encourage a horse to stay straight if he has a bad drift one way or another – see diagrams overleaf.

If a horse is careless or has poor technique it is very difficult to put right, but through jumping exercises you can, to a certain extent, improve a horse's style. For example, if a horse tends to dangle his front legs at uprights or leave his forearm down, you can sometimes improve his technique by jumping an oxer with a low cross rail in front, and gradually making the back pole higher and wider, so that the horse has to keep picking up his shoulder and forearm as the size of the jump increases. If the horse keeps knocking down an oxer, it can help to place a rail diagonally from a corner at the front to the opposite corner of the back rail. This has the effect of giving the jump a different look, so that when the horse approaches it his attention is drawn to it and he should make more effort over the fence.

Another way to help a horse that dangles his legs in front is to place a rail on the ground 1ft 6ins – 2ft (45–60cm) away from the base of an upright. This gives the horse a little security on the take-off and seems to help him.

When training a horse over show jumps I usually like him to wear open-

Using poles to keep a horse straight. Drawings (a) to (c) show pole positions for horses who drift to the left. To help horses who drift to the right, reverse the positions of the poles.

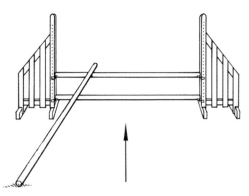

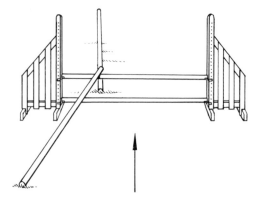

(a) If your horse drifts to the left, a pole placed like this can help to keep him straight. Also, use a right opening rein.

(b) A pole on the ground on the landing side can help to keep the horse straight if he drifts left on landing.

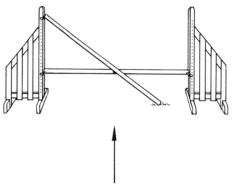

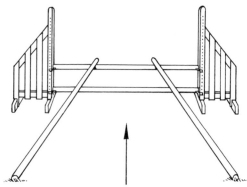

(c) A pole placed like this can also help to stop a left drift.

(d) Poles placed in a 'V' like this can help a horse stay straight when he tends to 'screw' over his fences. It is also useful for a horse who is a little careless with his front legs.

fronted boots so that if he does hit the fence he feels the full impact of it against his legs, and hopefully will learn from his mistake.

One thing that will encourage a horse to be careless is repeated jumping over the same obstacle. He will soon become bored and stop making an effort. Although it is a little more work for you, it pays to keep changing the jumps so that the horse is not doing the same exercise all the time.

Cross-country schooling

Before I do any cross-country jumping I like to tie a small knot in the end of my reins to shorten them. This avoids having a big loop of extra rein that could get caught under the saddle flap and interfere with your steering at a vital moment, and it also guards against the buckle coming undone, causing you to lose a rein midway round the course.

I like to ride quite short across country. It is easier to keep yourself in balance with the horse at the gallop if your weight is forward over the horse's centre of balance. Also, if you are having to pull against a horse that is quite strong and your stirrups are too long, your lower leg will swing forward and lose contact. You will then have less control of the horse and will bump up and down on his back, making it uncomfortable and tiring for him. With shorter stirrups you can get your weight down into the heel, keep the lower leg in contact with the horse and set your weight against him to hold him.

These pictures show the length of stirrup that I like to use for show jumping (left) and for the cross-country (right). The steeplechase length is two holes shorter than my cross-country length.

Your length of stirrup depends to some extent on your build and on the shape of your horse and how he goes. I normally go up two or three holes from my show-jumping position (which is already five holes shorter than

Jumping corners.

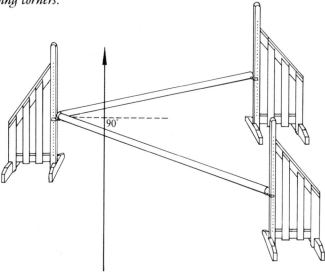

(a) Make a corner using three show-jump wings. Initially the wing on the corner will help to hold your horse on the correct line. Ideally, you should jump across the corner at 90° to an imaginary line that dissects the angle of the corner.

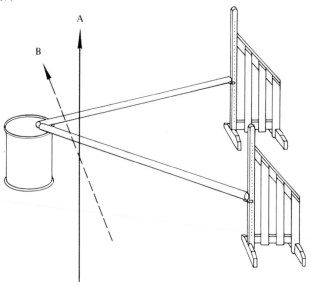

(b) Once the horse has become accustomed to jumping across a corner fence set out as above, replace the wing with a barrel or something similar, so that there is nothing to hold the horse on his line. You can also practise jumping the corner at different angles (line B, for example), which you may have to do in a competition. Remember to start off with low obstacles and with poles not too far apart. You can increase the angle between the poles to make the corner more difficult as your horse gains confidence.

my dressage length), and another two holes for the steeplechase. You should ride with your seat out of the saddle between the fences on the cross-country, but stay fairly low and close to the horse. You can then bring your seat into contact with the horse when you want to turn or balance him in front of a fence.

It is vitally important when riding across country to have the feeling that your horse is taking you forward into the fences. I do not mean that he should grab hold of the bit and race at each fence, rather that he should be in front of your leg, going into your hand. You must feel that you would have an immediate response if you asked the horse to go forward. If necessary kick him into a gallop, or use your stick. You should do this while you are warming him up, and not wait until you set out on a cross-country course, because if the horse is not going forward into your hand at that stage you will probably have a stop. Of course, this all relates back to your flat work, where your first concern was to teach your horse to go forward from the leg. This becomes even more important when you are riding across country.

It is also essential when riding across country to be able to keep a horse straight and to hold a line through several fences. If your horse has already learned to go straight on the flat, there should not be any problem. You must fix your eye on the line you want to take, keep the rhythm, come in straight to the fence and canter away again in a straight line. Once you have established this you can go on to practise over two or more fences, and then over fences at angles (not too acute for the novice horse), making sure that the horse stays straight all the way through the combinations.

One of the best riders in the world for holding a line through a fence is Ginny Leng. When she jumps a corner or goes through an angled combination she looks at the fence, lines it up and then rides her horse in a straight line from which she never deviates. She makes it look very easy, but it does not happen just like that. She has trained the horse to do it.

You can introduce a horse to cross-country type fences in your own field at home, using ordinary show jumps or rustic poles. Keep the fences very small, so that if your horse makes a mistake it will not worry him, and do not ask him to go too fast. Jumping corners is a good exercise in keeping a horse straight. There is no need to get yourself in a state about jumping corners. Just treat them as if you were jumping one side of a parallel, and fix your eye on the line.

You can set up a coffin-type fence by putting rails on the ground to imitate a ditch between two upright fences. You can also construct bounces, which normally range from 12ft–15ft (3.6m – 4.5m) on cross-country courses. Remember to keep the horse's rhythm as you approach a bounce and, again, keep him straight.

Once your horse is jumping confidently over small fences in the school or field it is a good idea to further his education by jumping a few logs while out hacking. We have quite a lot of logs of varying sizes around us, and I have found that they are very good obstacles for instilling confidence. When you are out hacking you can also introduce the horse to small ditches, if you have any in your area, or to water if you have a stream nearby, so that you gradually get him used to a wide variety of obstacles.

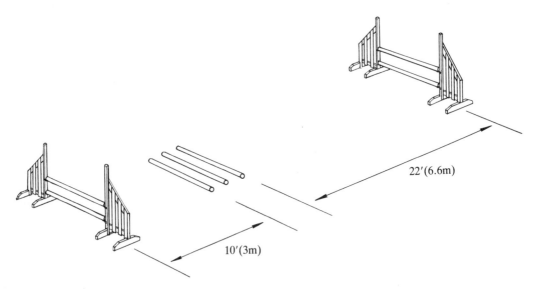

22'(6.6m)

10'(3m)

To introduce a horse to coffin-type fences you can set up your show jumps as shown here. The poles on the ground simulate a ditch. You could progress to using a water-tray instead of poles to make the horse 'look' a little. Build the combination so that you can jump it both ways.

When you first introduce a horse to water start off by asking him to walk into the water, and then walk around in it, so that he becomes confident about it. A horse is quite likely to try to turn away from it at first, but you must keep him facing the water and keep riding him forward until you get him in; then make a big fuss of him. Then walk him out and then back in again. Keep going until you can trot him in and out, and then, if the water is not too deep, canter him in and out. You can progress to introducing small obstacles into the water, gradually building them up so that the horse gains confidence and is not at all bothered about it. It is then a good idea to take him to several different water jumps, to make sure that he is happy about water wherever he meets it.

If all is going well, the next step is to take the horse to local jumping shows or cross-country schooling days over very small obstacles, so that he sees as many different types of fence as possible. At this early stage it is important that the fences are kept low, particularly if you are introducing the horse to solid cross-country obstacles. Then, if a horse does spook or stop at a fence you can kick him over from a standstill, so that he always learns to go forward. If you over-face a horse at this stage, and he learns to stop, it can be very difficult to get this out of the horse's mind.

The first couple of times that you go cross-country schooling, particularly if you are a novice yourself, make sure that someone experienced comes with you in case you run into problems. It can be useful if that person has a lunge whip nearby to give some assistance from the ground if you have serious difficulties in making a horse go over a fence. If you know a horse

Introducing a horse to his first cross-country obstacles. Small, natural obstacles, such as fallen trees, ditches and banks, offer a good education for a novice horse. The horse should learn that it is fun to jump natural obstacles, and if you keep them small to start with he will soon gain confidence.

is particularly spooky or hesitant then it makes sense to ask a rider on an experienced horse to give you a lead over a 'sticky' fence. If you do this at the beginning you will avoid the possibility of creating a problem early on in your cross-country training.

It takes only one or two sessions over small obstacles such as this for a horse to understand what is wanted. Later, when you take him cross-country schooling, you should not have any problems.

Your horse will progress much more quickly if you can take him away to as many different places as possible. He will learn far more than he would by staying at home in a familiar atmosphere, jumping the same things every day in your schooling area. Hunter trials and pre-novice one-day events are good starting places. The hunting field can also be a useful schooling ground for the young eventer as long as the horse is hunted sensibly. Anything of that nature is good experience for a novice horse, so that when you do finally take him to his first one-day event he has already had quite a broad education and is not completely fazed by finding himself in a competition atmosphere.

At his first events do not worry about getting your horse round inside the time. If you hurry a young, inexperienced horse you will teach him to race at his fences, and you may frighten him if you ask him to go too fast. Treat the first few events as training sessions to increase your horse's confidence, to get him going forward between hand and leg and to introduce him to as many different types of obstacles as possible. With a young horse I like to jump most of the difficult options, provided I feel he is ready, because he will learn more doing that than by always going the easy way. It does not matter if your horse makes a mistake, as long as he tries.

Problems in training

There are all sorts of problems that you may encounter in your training, some of them easier to deal with than others. If you strike a problem with your horse, try to think it through logically. Am I asking the horse correctly? Does he understand what is wanted? You need to be a bit of a psychologist to keep one step ahead of your horse.

It can be very frustrating training a young horse, particularly if you are not an experienced rider yourself and you are both learning together. It is very important to keep your cool and not to let things that the horse might do worry you unduly. If you can stay calm and objective then you can continue schooling a horse without letting him annoy you. Once you start getting angry you would be better to hop off and go and have a cup of tea, and then come back later. If you have a fight with a young horse he may lose trust in you, and you can set his training back several weeks.

It is important to gain the horse's trust from the outset. The best way to do this, particularly with a young horse, is to have a methodical training programme in which you are always building on the horse's education. Whilst you can continually ask him to do a little more, you should never ask him to do something that is going to destroy his faith in you. For example, the first time you take a horse on a cross-country training session do not point him straight at a difficult fence. If he stops, you will then have to take the whip out and beat him through it, and he is going to think: 'I don't like this. It's no fun.' You have to be firm with the horse and make him go over, because a young horse is bound to be a bit hesitant to start with. But if you begin over small obstacles he will not hurt himself if he does stop, and you can then make him jump from a standstill. It only takes one or two schooling sessions over small fences to get the horse going and for him to think: 'Wow, this is good fun.' Most horses that are going to be reasonably good will go on quickly from there, and it is just at that first introduction that you have to be extremely careful.

Pulling

No matter how carefully you break and school horses you are going to encounter some that are stronger than others and that pull or lean on you. If I have a young horse that is strong, I much prefer to put a sharper bit in his mouth early on rather than persevere with a snaffle and have the horse yanking and tugging at me, so that I then have to yank and tug back at him. When that happens the horse just gets harder in the mouth and learns to pull back at you. If you put him in a sharper bit earlier on, the horse learns to have a greater respect for the bit and you are more likely to be able to go back to a snaffle later.

Some horses pull naturally. With me it seems to go in runs. I had Charisma, Michaelmas Day and Welton Greylag, who all used to pull like fury. Then I got Bahlua, Jued Lad and Pedro, who did not pull at all. Whatever their quirks, my horses have the same basic workplan and they all do the same sort of training and fitness exercises, but with their individual needs in mind. I like to canter the lazy ones alongside another horse to make them a bit keener. I prefer to work the pullers on their own and try to switch them off so that they just lollop along off the bridle and learn to relax when they are cantering.

Michaelmas Day and Welton Greyleg are usually cantered in pelhams, and Michaelmas Day wears a pelham for cross-country. In their younger days these two horses were real tearaways at competitions. I used to experiment quite a lot with Michaelmas Day because I found that whenever I put a new bit on him it would work quite well for two or three runs, but then he would get the hang of it and it would lose its effectiveness, so I would have to try something else. Over the years he has become more mature, and no longer tries to run off between fences. He has always done his canter work in front of other horses or on his own, so that he has learned to switch off a bit, and this has now transferred itself to his competition behaviour. Now I can usually get him to calm down between fences, whereas before there used to be a battle between the fences and an even bigger battle as I approached each fence and tried to steady up.

Generally I prefer to school a lazy horse because it is really just a question of educating him to be obedient to the leg. What happens with a lot of lazy horses is that the riders just keep on kicking at them, and this makes a horse even more dead to the aids. When you ask the horse to go forward from the leg and nothing happens, you should give him a couple of good ones with the stick just behind the leg so that he then associates the stick with the leg. You must always ride a horse forward, no matter where he is or whether he has got his head in the air. You must make him go forward at all times so that he understands that when you put your leg on it means go forward.

Running out

If a horse runs out at fences this needs to be put right straight away. Running out is a problem normally associated with riders who do not keep the horse between hand and leg when coming into a fence and are therefore not keeping the horse straight.

To correct a horse that has run out always turn him back towards the fence. In other words, if he runs out to the left, turn him back to the right. Once you have re-organised yourself, get straight for the fence and present him again. Carry your stick in your left hand and use it down his left shoulder, but do not approach the fence too fast. The faster you go the easier it is for a horse to run out. In the early stages of introducing a horse to cross-country you should approach the fences quite slowly to give the horse more time to see what he is being asked to do, and then he is more likely to accept the situation. As long as the fences are low it is better sometimes to come in at a trot so that you have the horse firmly between your leg and hand and are much better able to keep the horse straight and moving forward.

Stopping

Horses who stop usually learn to do so either because the rider has not been strong enough at the outset so the horse has not learned to go forward over obstacles, or because he has been over-faced. Sometimes it is because the rider just does not keep enough leg on.

I might forgive a young horse for stopping once if he is very green and very spooky, but if he stops again he gets a good telling off with the stick so that he knows he has done something wrong. More often than not he will then go forward and will not repeat his mistake. If you let the horse stop again and again he learns to do it. You are much better off being really firm with him early on. If you think: 'Oh dear, poor baby, he doesn't understand what I want,' then you are letting the horse have the upper hand.

Water obstacles and ditches

If you have problems with ditches and water obstacles you have to decide whether a horse is genuinely frightened of the fence or whether he is just being naughty. If he is actually frightened then you must be very careful to go right back to the beginning and re-introduce your horse to this type of fence to gain his confidence again at that level. If he is just being disobedient, then now is the time to give him a good lesson. You should be very strong with the leg and stick, and make him understand that under no circumstances must he stop at this type of fence.

Sometimes, if a horse has just had a fright at water or a ditch you can go back and re-school him successfully, but if a horse is always spooky you may not be able to get it out of his system. You may find that, although you eventually persuade a horse to jump a particular ditch or water obstacle at home, every time you take him to a new obstacle you strike the same problem. Horses that behave in this way very seldom come right, and whilst you may get away with the problem up to a certain level, once the fences get bigger the horse's confidence evaporates and you run into trouble.

I certainly would not condemn a young horse straight away because he was a little spooky at water or ditches. Often he will just need a bit of repetitive schooling over that type of obstacle to gain his confidence, but if he does not begin to jump the fences more happily, you could have problems. I once had a novice horse that was always hesitant at ditches,

1

2

5

6

3   4

Introducing a young horse to water for the first time.

1. *The horse puts his ears back, his head up, and says: 'I don't want to go in there.' (Note that I am carrying a stick and wearing spurs, something I always do when cross-country schooling.)*
2. *It is important at this stage that you do not let the horse turn away. Keep urging him forward with only enough contact to keep him straight. He must know that he can go forward.*
3. *Suddenly the horse says: 'All right, I will go in.' You must still keep your leg on strongly, in case he changes his mind. Keep urging him forward into the water.*
4. *Keep him going until all four legs are in the water.*
5. *Once he is in, pat him and make a fuss of him; let him know that there is nothing to be afraid of.*
6. *Let him stand in the water and have a drink if he wants, so that he relaxes completely. Then repeat the exercise until the horse will walk or trot into the water without a moment's hesitation, all the time rewarding him with your voice and patting him when he does it correctly.*

This was the first time that this horse had ever been through water and he took to it very quickly. If your horse does not, then you must persevere until he gives in. Never let the horse turn away from the water. Sometimes you have to be quite strong with the leg and stick initially to persuade a horse to go in. If you anticipate having a problem, it is a good idea to have someone on the ground with a long stick to add his or her support. It can also help to have a more experienced horse to lead the way through the water the first time.

and although we schooled and schooled and schooled him, it made no difference. He managed the fences at novice level, but I knew that he was not going to make the grade because he simply wasn't brave enough.

Horses do need to be brave. Charisma, for example, was an exceptionally courageous horse. He received a tremendous ducking in the water at the World Championships in Gawler, yet without being schooled at water before his next event in Luhmühlen, he jumped straight into the two big water fences there without a moment's hesitation. That is the difference between a brave horse and one who lacks courage.

Shying

There is very little you can do about a horse who shies. If you beat him up when he shies at something, you usually end up with him associating whatever he was shying at with being beaten, so he will shy even more. You need to switch off, try to bend his head away from whatever he is looking at and just ride on as if there is nothing there. Some horses are persistent shiers, and although they do tend to grow out of it a bit, it is often a habit that you have to learn to put up with and not get too annoyed about.

CHAPTER 3　*Fitness*

If you are going to compete in horse trials, whether in one-day or three-day events, it is essential that your horse is fit enough to cope with the level of competition at which you will be aiming him. You cannot expect to get the best out of your horse if he is not fit, and you may even cause damage to his limbs or wind. Obviously, the level of fitness required varies a great deal between one-day events and three-day events, and also whether the horse is a youngster just starting off or an older horse that has already done a lot of competitive work.

In a normal season I like to start work with the horses either after Christmas or early in the New Year. If I have horses going to Badminton, which is the first major three-day event in the spring calendar, ideally they will come back into work in the middle of December so that they have a slightly longer preparation.

I always like to set out a programme for each horse building up to a three-day event, so that I have a firm idea of where I am heading and what I am going to do. But it is certainly not the be-all-and-end-all if, as often happens, something causes me to have to alter that programme. For one reason or another I may find it necessary to increase or decrease a horse's work, or I may strike a problem with an injury. However well planned your campaign is, you should be prepared to be flexible and to adjust your programme should the need arise.

A novice horse coming straight out of the field will be walked for about two weeks, whereas the older horses tend to be walked for longer – probably three to four weeks. This is because the level of fitness needed in the older horses will be much greater, as they will be competing at a higher level, so I like to spend longer in the walking stage, hardening up their legs before I ask them to do any more work. By doing that you are less likely to have problems with muscle and tendon strains at a later stage in the fitness programme. With the younger horses, even their flat work is not so demanding as that of the more advanced horses, so their whole fitness regime is much less tough.

At the beginning of the season, once the horse gets beyond the walking stage, he will need to be clipped out. For horses that are going to be doing a three-day event in the spring, such as Saumur or Badminton, I like to clip them out fully, including the saddle patch. I find that a horse gets sweaty in the saddle patch and if it is not thoroughly cleaned you can end up with a scurfy back, so it is easier to remove the whole lot.

For a novice horse, or one that is not doing a three-day event until later in the season, a trace clip is probably sufficient. In the damp winter months it is much easier to dry off a clipped horse after he has been working and it makes it more comfortable for the horse.

One thing that you must never underestimate is the part that schooling on the flat plays in the fitness programme of an event horse. I spend between twenty and thirty minutes schooling each novice horse, mostly doing basic dressage training but also incorporating some simple jumping exercises, and they also go for a hack. What they do out hacking will depend on their level of fitness, but once they are reasonably fit they will do quite a lot of trotting and a bit of hill work to build up their strength and balance.

If you cannot school your horse very often, the hacking will need to be more demanding to make up for the lack of work in the school. The horse can be taken out for longer and worked harder, perhaps with some canter work and a few schooling exercises incorporated into the hack, but for the novice horse, his total work time never exceeds $1\frac{1}{2}$ hours. For example, if I school a horse for 30 minutes, he is then hacked quietly for 45 minutes to an hour, but if I had schooled a horse hard for 40 minutes and he had also worked hard the previous day, I might do no other work with him that day.

All my horses are worked six days a week and have one rest day. They usually have four days' schooling (plus a hack), and two days of canter work. Once they start competing they are always given a day off after an event, and then probably go for a gentle hack on the following day.

On the days that I school the more advanced horses they go out for a hack for about an hour and a half. They do not hack for longer than that unless I have been unable to school them. I do not think it is necessary for a horse to be out for too long. If I want them to work harder then they can trot for most of that time, or they can do more hill work. An hour and a half is quite long enough for a horse to be working; if you cannot do the work you want to in that time I do not think that prolonging the hack is going to help. The actual speed and endurance test does not take much longer than an hour and a half so there is no point hacking your horse for hours on end.

I like to vary the horses' routines as much as possible so that they do not fall into the habit of thinking that they are always, say, going for a hack before they do their schooling work. Some days they will come straight out of the stable and do their schooling, as they would if they were at a competition. They must learn that if they are going out to school they have got to knuckle down and concentrate on their work. Some horses, however, work much better after they have been hacked. Michaelmas Day is one of these. He tends to be rather excitable and can sometimes be a bit stiff on one side, so on competition days I always get someone to hack him out for about an hour before I get on to do my preparation for the dressage test. At home, though, he still goes straight into the school on some days, so that he knows he has to do that.

You also want to vary the daily timetable so that your horse learns to be reasonably flexible. At competitions you may be required to do your

I like my horses to go out for at least two hours every day, if possible. In wet or cold weather they always wear their New Zealand rugs.

dressage in the afternoon, and if your horse is used to being worked only in the morning, he may, if he is the super-sensitive type, become upset when he suddenly has to do his work in the afternoon. I find anyway that, particularly with my novice horses, their work has to fit in with what I am doing on a particular day, because the horses being prepared for major three-day events must take precedence. I always try to adhere to their training and fitness schedules, and fit the novices in around them. Whatever happens, though, I like to keep all the horses' feed times regular.

If the weather is reasonable, I like the horses to go out every day for two or three hours. On their day off they go out in the morning and spend all day in the field. I think it is very important for horses to go out. They are much healthier in their natural environment, and you are less likely to get problems with their general health, and particularly their respiration, if they can live out in the field.

It is also good for them mentally, as it keeps them slightly more sane. If they are cooped up in a stable all day they can develop problems such as weaving and wind-sucking. Horses that are a bit hyped up can often benefit from being left out all day, as it helps them to unwind. We turn ours out in groups of two to five, and because they are used to going out every day we have very few problems with horses being kicked. You soon learn if two horses do not get on, or if you have one that is a bit difficult, and you just shuffle them around.

Obviously, with the large number of horses that we have in our yard it is much easier to control their condition if they are stabled, but I certainly do not think it does any harm for a novice horse to be kept out during the day, or, during the summer when the flies are bad, to be kept in during the day and turned out all night. The only thing you should watch is that they do not have an abundance of grass to eat, as that may be detrimental to their general fitness. In New Zealand we used to train our event horses out of the field, and a lot of racehorses are trained out of the field quite successfully.

Monitoring fitness

For some people, monitoring a horse's fitness has become an exact art. I tend to do it mostly by feel, doing whatever seems right for each horse, rather than relying on taking pulse and respiration rates all the time. A horse doing novice one-day events does not need to be tremendously fit. If he is doing regular work five or six days a week for 1–1½ hours, and is in reasonable condition physically, then he will probably be fit enough to do a novice one-day event. Obviously if the horse is very fat you will have to do stronger work to get that horse's weight down so that he is in a condition to compete even at a one-day horse trial, otherwise you risk heart strain, muscle strain and tendon strain.

The work that you do in getting a five- or six-year-old to his first one-day event – i.e. building up different types of muscle so that he can do the job – will probably result in him being fit enough to cope with the distance and speed of a novice cross-country course. I find that I do not actually have to work on fitness as such with my novice horses because the training they do is enough to ensure a reasonable level of fitness in the early stages.

You will gain an idea of how fit your horse is if you go cross-country schooling, as you can see how quickly he recovers after he has jumped some fences, or after a fast canter. When you school a horse on the flat for twenty minutes, if he blows a lot or finds it quite difficult to do the work, then you know you must do more to get him fit. If you hunt, then you will already have a fair idea of how fit a horse needs to be.

Before a novice horse tackles his first one-day event, he should have been out to several little show-jumping competitions, and have been taken for some cross-country training. He should also have been given several fitness-type canters to get him used to cantering at a faster speed than a normal dressage-type canter. You need to get a horse used to cantering outdoors in a field so that he learns to go along on his own in open spaces. This is particularly important if most of your basic training work is done in an indoor school. In the early stages you are trying to lay down as broad a base of education for the horse as possible by taking him on training days and by taking him out and about, exposing him to other horses and to different environments.

Each competition should bring the horse's fitness on a bit more. Once he has done two or three his muscles will be that much harder, and as long as you keep the work going he will become fitter and fitter. One of the

Bahlua and Michaelmas Day ease up towards the end of their canter work.

hardest things is to bring a horse that is just broken-in to a stage where his muscles are strong enough to do an event. Once you have had a horse fit it is much easier to get him fit again.

Fitness programme for a three-day event

Getting a horse fit for a three-day event is a more exacting task. I start off with three or four weeks' walking, building in periods of trotting in the last week – for example, walking for ten minutes, trotting for three minutes, then gradually increasing the length of time spent in trotting. After about a month I normally start to do a little schooling with the horses. For the first week this concentrates on: asking the horse to go in a regular rhythm with a fairly long, low outline; making the horse relax; and getting him used to accepting the leg again. I work through the basic walk, trot and canter movements without asking for too much engagement or too much effort from the horse.

I probably school only three times a week to start with (see fitness plan). After that, depending on how the horse is going, I start to ask for more in the schooling. The horse should become more energetic in his work, and produce more impulsion. But this would be done gradually, not suddenly and for a long period. I might ask for five minutes of stronger work, and then allow the horse to relax again, so that I am gradually building up the horse's muscle tone. Whether he is schooling on the flat or jumping and galloping, the horse needs to build up the muscles to do these things correctly, and this cannot be done overnight. It is a gradual process.

You will soon know if you have over-done it, as the horse will become very tired or slightly distressed. On the other hand, if the horse is not working up a sweat and not showing signs of working, then you could increase the amount you are doing or make him work harder.

By the end of six to eight weeks the horses are becoming reasonably fit, and you can gradually start introducing some canter work. The time spent on this depends a great deal on your location and on what facilities are available for your use. I usually canter the horses twice a week, on a Tuesday and a Saturday, so that the work is spaced out, and they are given Sunday off. At Cholderton we used to take the horses to Salisbury Plain, where the terrain allowed us to have two or three canters of varying lengths. One canter took three minutes, another one five minutes and another seven minutes. They were all up hill, and some had steeper parts.

I think this is the ideal situation because you can make a horse work quite hard without doing a lot of mileage, whereas if you are trying to get a horse fit on totally flat ground you have to cover greater distances, which means more wear and tear on the horse to achieve the same result. Another advantage of hillwork is that it tends to make a horse blow and therefore to use his lungs more, so that lung capacity is increased. Again, if you are working on the flat you have to do faster work to achieve the same result, which puts more strain on the horse's legs. It is possible to train a horse for three-day eventing on flat land, but it is certainly much easier if you are able to work on hills.

When your horse first starts canter work he should be ready to do a three-minute canter twice in the first week. In the second week that might be increased to a four-minute and a five-minute canter, and in the third week these could be followed by a third canter of three minutes, with a five-minute walk between each canter. Gradually build up the amount of work until the horse is able to do all three canters.

This is a basic plan for an older horse coming up from grass and preparing for a three-day event. When making a plan it is easier to start with the final goal and work backwards, filling in the lead-up competitions and then fitting the workplan around them. You can vary the work to fit in with your eventing programme.

Be prepared to be flexible. You will almost certainly have to alter your plans for some reason, perhaps because of injury to the horse or cancellation of events.

A horse coming up from grass for one-day eventing would follow the same basic routine up to his first one-day event, though the length of time spent schooling and hacking would be slightly reduced. After the first competition the horse would be kept on a 'maintenance' programme, similar to his previous routine, rather than continuing to have his workload increased. Young horses, like younger people, hold their fitness better, so they do not need to be worked hard between competitions.

EXAMPLE FITNESS PLAN

	MONDAY	TUESDAY	WEDNESDAY	THURSDAY	FRIDAY	SATURDAY	SUNDAY
Wk 1	Walk 1 hr	Walk 1 hr	Walk 1 hr	Walk 1 hr	Walk 1¼ hr	Walk 1¼ hr	Rest
Wk 2	Walk 1¼ hr	Walk 1¼ hr	Walk 1½ hr	Walk 1½ hr	Walk 1½ hr	Walk 1¾ hr	Rest
Wk 3	Walk 1¾ hr	Walk 2 hr	Walk 2 hr	Walk 2 hr	Walk 1¾ hr Some short trots	Walk 1¾ hr Short trots	Rest
Wk 4	Walk 1½ hr Short trots	Hack 1½ hr Increased trots	Hack 1½ hr Increased trots	Hack 1½ hr Increased trots	Light school 20 mins Quiet hack 1 hr mostly walking	Same as Friday	Rest
Wk 5	Hack 1½ hr	School 30 mins Hack 1 hr	Hack 1½ hr Some hills	School 30 mins Hack 1 hr	Same as Wednesday	Same as Wednesday	Rest
Wk 6	Hack 1½ hr	School 30/40 mins (flat and jump) Hack 1¼ hr	School 30/40 mins Hack 1¼ hr	Hack 1½ hr Hillwork	Same as Tuesday	Same as Friday	Rest
Wk 7	Hack 1½ hr	Hack 1 hr include 3 min uphill canter	School 20 mins Hack 1 hr	School 30 mins Hack 1¼ hr	School 40 mins Hack 1¼ hr	Same as Tuesday	Rest
Wk 8	School 30 mins Hack 1¼ hr	Hack include 4 min canter	School 20 mins Hack 1¼ hr	School 40 mins Hack 1¼ hr	Same as Thursday	Hack include 5 min canter	Rest
Wk 9	School 30 mins Hack 1¼ hr	Hack & canter 3×3 mins 3 min walk between	Quiet hack 1½ hr	Show jumping	School 40 mins Hack 1¼ hr	Canter 3 & 4 mins	Dressage day
Wk 10	Rest	School 30 mins Hack 1 hr	Canter 4×5 mins	Quiet hack 1¼ hr	School 40 mins Hack 1¼ hr	Show jumping	Canter 5×5 mins
Wk 11	Rest	School 30 mins Hack ¼ hr	Canter 5×7	School 20 mins Hack 1 hr	School 40 mins Hack 1¼ hr	One-day event Quiet run	Rest
Wk 12	Quiet hack 1¼ hr	School 40 mins Hack 1½ hr	Canter 5×3×5 mins	School 30 mins Walk 1½ hr	School 40 mins Hillwork 1¼ hr	School 30 mins Hack 1½ hr	One-day event
Wk 13	Rest	Quiet hack 1½ hr	School 30/40 mins Hack 1½ hr	Canter 3×7×5 mins	School 20 mins Quiet hack 1½ hr	School 30/40 mins Hack 1½ hr	Canter 3×7×5 mins
Wk 14	Rest	School 30 mins Hack 1½ hr	Canter 7×5 mins last 2 mins stronger	School 20 mins Hack 1½ hr	School 20 mins Canter 7×5 mins	School 30 mins Quiet hack 1¼ hr	One-day event
Wk 15	Rest	Quiet hack 1½ hr	Canter 7×5 mins	School 30/40 mins Quiet hack 1 hr	Same as Thursday	Strong gallop 1 mile (1.6km)	Rest
Wk 16	School 30 mins Walk 1¼ hr	Gallop early if needed – otherwise hack Travel to event	Vet inspection Quiet hack or school	DRESSAGE	**THREE – DAY EVENT** DRESSAGE	X-C DAY	SHOW JUMPING

When our horses are close to peak fitness they have a ten-minute walk and trot before their first canter; then they do a fairly steady canter on flat ground for about five minutes; then they have a long canter, which takes about seven or eight minutes, and the last part of that is up quite a good pull. They then walk for about five minutes, before cantering back to where we started. A fifteen- to twenty-minute walk home ensures that they have stopped blowing and cooled down by the time they get back to the stables.

The amount of work you need to do also depends to a certain extent on the sort of horse you have. I find that Thoroughbreds become fit more easily than part-bred horses, but you can sometimes encounter a lazy Thoroughbred. A horse with a keen attitude is easier to get fit because he works harder, whereas a lazy horse does not put as much effort into his training and you have to chase him to make him work well. Wilton Fair, on whom I won Burghley in 1987, was a fairly lazy horse; cantering him on his own was hard work for the rider. I used to canter him with another horse to try to make him keener, and I always carried a stick to encourage him to work up into the bridle. You have to watch that your horse does not just idle along when he is cantering. Make him work into his bridle just as you would in his flat work.

Bahlua doing steady canter work, but still being kept up to the bit. If much of your training has been done in a school you will need to make sure that your horse is willing to canter along on his own in wide open spaces. Some horses need to be taught to do this.

Some horses are a little thick in the wind and blow a lot when they are doing fast work, and this can mean that they have excess fat around their lungs. Horses that are fat to start with often retain fat inside their body after they have lost weight elsewhere, so you have to make sure that you have got rid of it if you want a really fit horse. A good example of this was Charisma who was always quite stuffy in his wind, and he needed several good runs to really blow himself out and clear his lungs.

Charisma was a difficult horse to get fit, despite the fact that he always used to pull like a train in his canter work. He needed to work off some of his body fat (his stable name was 'Podge') and he also had problems with his sinuses, which gave him a permanent slight nasal discharge. I had to keep him in a dust-free environment and he needed a lot more work than some horses. As he grew older, it took him even longer to reach peak fitness. This is quite normal – horses over the age of twelve tend to need more work than eight- and nine-year-olds.

As part of their fitness programme my horses will do two or three one-day events. This is one time when I do study carefully the horse's recovery rate to see how long it takes for the respiration to return to normal at the end of the cross-country. I look at my watch when I finish the course and then five minutes later check the horse to see how much he is blowing.

After a couple of runs in one-day events you will have fair idea of how your horse's fitness is progressing. If he is still blowing a lot at the end of the cross-country, you may need to give him a couple of good strong gallops at home. If the horse gets tired half way round the cross-country course then you should probably step up the work a bit. Provided that you have a good base to your horse's fitness, and you have put in the longer, slower work in the beginning, you can build on that base. If you have to hurry the fitness programme, then you are more likely to run into problems.

The number of one-day events a horse takes part in before a three-day competition depends on the horse. Some horses go better when they are a little fresh, others go better when they have had two or three runs. If a horse is not very experienced you may want to give him more outings to increase his confidence before he tackles a big event. Horses need competitions to put extra pressure on them, to make them exert themselves that much more, and to bring out the best in their fitness. A competition atmosphere also helps to sharpen them up mentally. It is the same with a rider. He also needs competitions to keep himself sharp.

It takes time and experience to learn how to bring a horse to peak fitness and to recognise when you have achieved it. Unfortunately, I cannot say do this, this and this, and you will have a fit horse. You have to learn to judge for yourself. But once a horse is really fit he will not need such long periods of work to keep him at his peak, so you should lighten up on the workload a bit. If you continue to train hard you can push a horse over the top, with the result that you make him sour.

Once a horse is fully fit he will feel tremendously well underneath you. His coat will look sleek and shiny; he will have a bright eye; he will revel in his work and eat up well; and even if he is lazy, when you go out for a hack and turn for home he might put in a little squeal and a buck. If you work the horse every day yourself you will learn to recognise these signs, and you will also know if the horse is not feeling quite right.

A week before the speed and endurance day of a three-day event I like to give a horse a good, strong gallop over about a mile (1.6km). This does not mean galloping flat out on a loose rein, kicking all the way; rather the horse is asked to gallop strongly whilst keeping him balanced.

Surprisingly, most horses need to be taught how to gallop properly, even some Thoroughbreds. Many riders never actually make their horses truly gallop. They do what I would call a threequarter pace, where they are going slightly faster than cross-country speed, but they are not actually at full-stretch gallop.

Horses need to learn to gallop properly so that when they arrive at a three-day event they find that the rate at which they have to go is like a cruising speed. This is the advantage of having a fast horse: he is never fully extended at the speed you have to do for a three-day event, so he finds it relatively easy and it takes much less out of him. This means that you can keep within the time more easily and your horse is going to be less exhausted and less stressed when he comes out on the final day.

The best way to teach a horse to gallop well is to run him with another horse. Wilton Fair did not have a good gallop. He was not a full Thoroughbred and had to learn to fully extend himself. I used to work him with other horses, particularly fast ones like Charisma, so that he had to be competitive and try to keep up. He did eventually learn to gallop reasonably well, though he was never destined to be a very fast horse.

The gallop on the Saturday before a three-day event helps to clear the horse's wind and sharpen him up for the competition. After that I will ease up on his work. You are not trying to get him any fitter at this stage; he should be fit enough by now. You should do just enough to keep his muscles in tone and to keep him sane in the mind, so that he will go into a major competition feeling on good form.

It is best to take your horse to a three-day event the day before the first horse inspection, but when long journeys are involved (e.g. to foreign events) I may arrive a day earlier to give the horses more time to get over the journey. The routine is much the same whether the event is in this country or overseas, though obviously if the horses have been travelling a long way they may have stiffened up a bit, or be feeling under the weather from the journey. Once you have arrived, lead the horse around for about twenty minutes to stretch his legs, and then let him settle down in the stable. If there is time later on in the day, you can take him for a quiet hack and let him have a look at the surroundings. On the Wednesday, the day of the first inspection (assuming the event starts on a Thursday), you can hack out again and perhaps do some schooling.

The amount of work you do will depend on how fresh the horse is feeling. If the horse is a bit of a worrier and does not travel very well, he can take a while to recover from a long journey. Welton Greylag was an anxious type initially, but he has improved with experience, whereas Charisma was never affected by a long journey because he was always so relaxed about it all. Your horse will generally let you know how he feels. If he is lying down a lot and seems lethargic then it is better not to work him too soon. You will be the best judge of how your horse is feeling and how much work he needs. The worst thing that you can do is work your horse when he is not really feeling up to it.

If, on the other hand, your horse is feeling full of himself you might give him a quiet canter at the event just to take the edge off him. You want him to go into a competition feeling a little on the fresh side but not so excitable that he is going to blow up in the dressage.

After the dressage I normally give the horse a pipe-opener, about half a mile at quite a fast gallop. I do not know if this has any beneficial effect, but it is a ritual that I go through. I honestly do not think it would make any difference to the horse whether I did it or not, but I like to think it helps.

Setbacks in fitness programmes

It is important to be conscious of the way your horse is going and how he feels all the time that you are training him. If you ride him every day you will usually notice if something is wrong, and you can often nip a problem in the bud. Sometimes, when I have been away at a competition and come back and ride one of my horses, I might think that the horse does not feel right. I will want to know what he has been eating and what he has been doing to see if there is any obvious reason why he is not feeling as he should. I may even have a blood test taken.

The most feared injury in training a horse for a three-day event is a damaged tendon. A serious strain could result in the horse being laid off work for most of the year. The important thing is to be on the look-out for signs of damage, so that any problems can be treated immediately before they develop into a more serious injury. It is a good idea to check your horse's legs every morning and night so that you know what their normal temperature is and whether there is any regular variation. Some horses' legs have a tendency to be slightly warmer in the afternoon, and they can also be affected by external temperature.

As a general rule, if you notice anything out of the ordinary – if the horse's leg has some heat or if there is some filling that is not usually there – stop work immediately. The worst thing that you can do is to carry on regardless in the hope that it might go away because, even if there was not a serious problem there in the first place, you will more than likely make it into one. When you are building up for a major competition that is, maybe, a month away, the hardest thing to do is to say to yourself: 'This horse is not going to make it and if I carry on I'm going to do more damage.' A lot of people decide to risk the horse, but nine times out of ten they create a more serious problem.

If I notice any swelling in one of my horse's legs and I cannot easily identify the cause, I call the vet straight away to try to diagnose the problem. If I am at all worried I might have the horse's leg scanned at this stage, as this will show if there is any damage to the horse's tendon and remove any doubt as to whether or not I can continue working the horse. If there is only slight heat in the leg it may disperse of its own accord a couple of days later – the horse might have knocked himself, or perhaps his diet has caused his legs to swell. In any case, it is sensible to stop work, cut down the feed, and just lead the horse out in hand for half an hour a couple of times a day and see what happens to the leg. If it rights itself within a day or two you can consider putting the horse back into light work. If there is any strain or sprain there, or any bow in the tendon, then the heat will not disappear for quite some time and you are looking at a minimum of six months off work.

I have reservations about the use of support bandages to prevent damage to the legs. The sheer weight of the horse pounding on his legs is so great that I do not think that wearing bandages is going to make much difference when he is working. Also, if the bandages are put on incorrectly, they are likely to cause damage to the horse's leg. There are a couple of horses in my yard that have had previous leg problems, but even with them I do not use support bandages. All my horses wear protective boots during exercise and at competitions, and that is all.

There are various lotions and potions for treating swollen legs. I find kaolin poultices very good for taking heat and filling out of a horse's legs. Cold water is also useful: you can run a hose down the leg, or use Wurly boots or ice-packs. If your horse has damaged a tendon it is very important that you put ice on to it as soon as possible to minimise the amount of swelling in the leg, as this latter causes even more damage to the tendon. I am not a great believer in total immobility, but if the horse has a bowed tendon and is very lame it is not a good idea to move him. Otherwise, I like a horse to be led out and allowed to stretch his legs. This helps to

A horse standing quietly in a pair of Wurly boots.

Another type of water boot. This one is attached to a hose, from which a spray of water runs down the horse's legs.

keep the blood circulating, which in turn helps to speed up the healing process.

I have found that the best treatment for heat and filling, or any suspicion of a sprained tendon, is to keep the legs cold with ice and water for as long as possible. This may mean alternating ice and pressure bandages on the horse's leg for a period of up to three weeks. When applying the ice, do not put it directly against the horse's skin as it can cause burning. It is also important to have a very good bandage to support the tendon when there is no ice on the leg.

A sprained tendon can be the result of overworking a horse, but it is often caused by a horse knocking into himself or tweaking his leg on unlevel ground, just as we might sprain an ankle. If a horse is going to have serious tendon trouble, in most cases you get some sort of warning. It is very unusual for a horse to break down without warning, but it can happen in a competition. I once rode a horse who broke down at an event

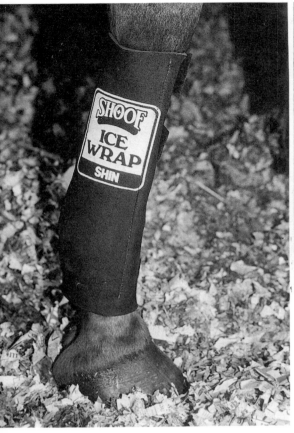

(left) *One of the types of ice boot available. These are attached to the horse's legs by velcro and have pockets inside to hold ice-packs against the horse's legs.* (above) *A much cheaper, but equally effective, way of applying ice. Once frozen, these ice-cube bags can be bandaged on to the horse's leg. The ice should not be placed directly against the horse's skin as it may cause burning.*

when there had been nothing wrong with him beforehand: he landed badly from a fence and bowed his tendon.

Muscle damage is a fairly common problem, but if the horse's workload is built up gradually, slowly strengthening his muscles and not asking him to do anything that he is not fit to do, you will cut down on the amount of muscle injuries. Tearing a muscle in the back or hindquarters can result in the horse being off work for several months, but if it is just a case of tweaking a muscle the horse should recover reasonably quickly. As a general rule, rest is the best cure for any injury, but there are various laser and ultrasonic machines that can help speed up the recovery rate.

When I was in New Zealand, we had a swimming pool nearby in which I used to swim the horses a lot, but I have never actually had a case where swimming would be particularly beneficial. It can be useful when, for example, a horse has an abscess in the foot and he is lame but there is nothing else wrong with him. If the horse is at a stage in his training programme when it is important for him to be kept in work then swimming can be the answer.

If the ground is very hard you can put pads under the horse's shoes to ease the jarring on his legs. The most important thing, though, is to find a

A horse with a magneta pulse blanket. This is a very useful, but expensive, piece of equipment. It sends electrical impulses into the horse's muscles to help them to relax. Primarily used to ease back pain and muscle tightness, but it can also be used on a horse's legs.

suitable place to train. Try to use an arena with a soft surface for schooling, and for canter work maybe go to a nearby racehorse trainer who has an all-weather gallop. You should work your horse as little as possible on rock hard ground. Once my horses have done their initial four to six weeks' road work, I try to stay off the roads as much as possible and ride on grass verges or on the Downs, so that they are not always hammering along on a hard surface. You put more wear and tear on their joints and legs if you are on roads all the time.

As a general rule, particularly for people who may be preparing for their first three-day event, it is a good idea to have a horse blood-tested at regular intervals to make sure that his system is in good shape. You can test for almost anything: dehydration, vitamin deficiency, mineral imbalance, haemaglobin count, or the presence of a virus.

The first test could be done fairly soon after the horse comes into work, and then another test or two could be taken during the preparations leading up to the three-day event, with the final test a week to ten days before the actual competiton. Hopefully the results will show improving fitness and condition in the horse, and it is useful to keep these results to compare with other blood tests that will be taken when preparing the same horse for future three-day events. As well as providing a fitness guide the tests can alert you to any health problems.

Other setbacks that you may encounter when getting a horse fit include azoturia, a stiffening of the muscles in the loins and hindquarters. This is usually caused by mis-management, when the horse has not been fed correctly for the amount of work that he is doing; but some horses do seem to be more prone to tying up than others. It is sometimes related to a selenium deficiency in the horse, which can be improved by feeding a vitamin supplement containing selenium. Putting a tablespoon of bicarbonate of soda in the horse's evening feed also seems to help. Again, a blood test should reveal a deficiency.

At any stage in the horse's fitness programme it is not going to hurt if the horse has two or three days, or even a week, off work. The horse will not become unfit in that time, though anything over a week might cause the horse to start losing some fitness. People tend to think that they cannot miss a single day's exercise, particularly when they are getting a horse ready for a three-day event. But it does not work that way, and it is better to give the horse a couple of days off to let it get over a minor injury than try to rush him back into work too quickly and aggravate the problem.

CHAPTER 4 *Feeding*

There are many different types of food available and theories abound on what a horse should eat. As a result the whole business of feeding can become over-complex and confusing. Basically the aim is to give the horse a balanced diet and provide him with the right quantity of food according to the amount of work that he is doing and his condition.

For horses competing at novice one-day event level specially formulated performance nuts or mixed feeds should be adequate. It is possible to prepare a horse for a three-day event solely on these, but I prefer to feed the three-day horses on a diet consisting mainly of straight oats (bruised). In New Zealand we used to have our own oat crusher and could prepare the oats as we needed them, which meant that they were much fresher. Usually, though, oats are sold ready crushed, so if possible try not to store them for too long. Old chest freezers make very good storage bins for feedstuffs. They are totally rat-proof and you can usually buy them quite cheaply.

Oats are the basis of the feed for our three-day event horses, and the rest is made up with either nuts, mixed feeds or perhaps some micronised (i.e. cooked) barley, and chaff. We give the horses a general vitamin supplement and they also have bran a couple of times a week. They all have salt licks in their stables.

The amount of hay I feed depends on the horse. A horse that is on the light side will have hay on offer whenever he is in the stable. This is given out two or three times a day so that the hay is kept as fresh as possible. A gross horse will obviously have to have his hay ration restricted. He can make you feel pretty mean about this, but it is for his own benefit.

I do not change the hay ration before a competition, though I would not give a horse a huge haynet just before his work. As a general rule, I don't give a horse anything to eat less than four hours before he goes cross-country at a three-day event.

It is worth spending extra money on buying good-quality hay. If your horse develops a cough it can sometimes be caused by dusty feed, and you might need to dampen or soak the horse's hay, or even put him on to hayage (silage for horses).

The amount you feed a horse when it first comes back into work will depend on his condition. If the horse is grossly overweight, for example, he will certainly not need much food initially, but if he comes in a bit thin you may need to give him the sort of food that will help him gain weight, such as boiled barley and sugar-beet. As the work increases you should

Mixing up feeds for the horses. Old chest freezers can be an effective and cheap way of storing foodstuffs to keep them safe from vermin.

gradually increase the protein ration, i.e. start feeding more oats. But, again, the amount of protein you feed depends to some extent on the horse. If he is a very excitable animal, it is not a good idea to feed oats, and you could keep him on less high-powered feeds such as nuts. Thus the sample diets shown in the feed table provided can only be taken as a rough guideline to the amounts a horse will need at each stage in his training. Each animal will differ slightly in his requirements.

On a horse's day off, when he is turned out in the field, I cut his feed in half and do not give him a midday feed.

I like to give the horses a bran mash with their night feed a couple of times a week. In the winter, or if a horse is in poor condition I like to replace the micronised barley with boiled barley. The young horses might also get soaked sugar-beet with their feed, but I never feed it to the three-day event horses in the last few weeks before a competition.

If a horse starts leaving his food I immediately cut back the amount I am feeding and perhaps reduce his workload until his appetite returns. Then I gradually start to increase the feed again. Loss of appetite can sometimes mean that you are actually feeding too much. As a horse nears peak fitness he may not want as much food as he did before, because as a horse becomes fitter, his stomach can shrink a little. The worst thing that you

Filling a large container used for soaking hay.

can do to a picky eater is to shove huge amounts of food in front of him in the hope that he will eat it. That can put a horse off his feed more than anything else. You would do better to cut the feed right back until he starts cleaning it up, and then gradually build up the amount again.

If a horse has not eaten his feed after about half an hour, particularly with his breakfast or midday meal, then take it away. You might have to experiment. If your horse is a fussy eater he may not like certain things, and you will have to discover his likes and dislikes. It can be helpful to feed a picky horse next to a horse who is a good eater so that he then has to become a little competitive about his food. You can also try giving the horse a vitamin supplement (B-group vitamins) to help stimulate his appetite.

Loss of appetite can sometimes indicate that a horse is unwell. If the horse loses his appetite and looks a bit dopey, it might pay to call the vet in to see if there is anything wrong. He may have a virus brewing.

About a month before a three-day event my horses usually have a night feed at 9 pm as well as their three feeds during the day. This is so that I can increase their food intake a little without increasing the size of their original feeds, which might put them off. If a horse is leaving any of his feed, it can help to cut down the size of the meal but give him a fourth feed instead.

EXAMPLE FEED CHARTS FOR A VARIETY OF EVENT HORSES

DESCRIPTION OF INDIVIDUAL	MORNING (scoops)	LUNCH (scoops)	EVENING (scoops)
Horse in full work before a three-day event	1 oats 1 coarse mix	1 oats ½ event cubes 1 coarse mix	2 oats 1 coarse mix 1 lucerne chaff
Excitable horse, good eater but doesn't hold condition very well	1 micronised barley ½ event cubes 1 coarse mix	1 oats ½ event cubes 1 coarse mix 1 lucerne chaff	1 micronised barley 1 event cubes 1 coarse mix 1 lucerne chaff
Novice horse competing in one-day events	½ micronised barley 1 coarse mix	1 event cubes 1 coarse mix	1 micronised barley ½ event cubes 1 lucerne chaff
Horse just starting work	1 micronised barley ½ coarse mix	1 micronised barley 1 event cubes	1 micronised barley 1 coarse mix 1 lucerne chaff

Note: *Weight per scoop (rough guide)*
Oats = $2\frac{3}{4}$ lbs/1.25 kg　　　　Coarse mix = $2\frac{1}{4}$ lbs/1 kg
Micronised barley = $2\frac{3}{4}$ lbs/1.25 kg　　Cubes = $3\frac{1}{4}$ lbs/1.5 kg

Feeding on long journeys

When travelling horses on long trips it is very important to give them plenty of water. They can easily become dehydrated on a journey, so keep offering them water and also give them some electrolytes. If your horse is very fussy it may be wise to take a couple of containers of the water that he is used to at home, as different-tasting water can be off-putting. Some people go to the trouble of adding molasses to the water at home so that when they arrive in another country where the water might taste slightly different, they just add some molasses and their horse cannot tell the difference. I have usually found that if a horse is thirsty he will drink water, whatever it tastes like.

It is a good idea to give your horse a bran mash before leaving, and to keep the feeds fairly light and regular on the journey, adding a little bran.

Your horse will be standing still for a long time, so if you can keep his bowels moving then his legs will not fill up quite so much. If the lorry you are travelling in is full, it is useful to make up the horse's feeds before you leave and seal them in separate bags stowed in a reasonably accessible place. Then you will not have to scavenge around trying to find all the ingredients to make up a feed. Give the horse plenty of hay so that he keeps eating and his digestive system is kept working.

I always carry a first-aid kit on the lorry, and something for the treatment of colic, just in case. If you are on a ferry and your horse gets colic, you cannot take him out of the box and walk him around, so you need to be able to give him some sort of relaxant and pain killer so that you can at least get him safely to shore before the colic becomes too serious. Horses have been known to die of colic on long ferry journeys.

CHAPTER 5   *Preparation of the Rider*

Fitness

It is surprising how many people forget that the rider, as well as the horse, needs to be fit for eventing. If your muscles are not well prepared, your riding will be affected: you will not be strong enough to ride a good dressage test; you will not have a strong seat for the cross-country and will be more likely to fall off, and if you do fall when you are not fit you are more likely to hurt yourself; you will also be very tired by the end of the course and therefore not able to offer your horse much help. At a three-day event you could find that you are even stiffer than your horse for the show jumping on the final day.

At the beginning of each season I normally go to a gymnasium to work-out two or three times a week, just to get my muscles into shape before I start doing a lot of work with the horses. Once the horses are in training I find that, because I am riding five, six, or even seven horses a day, including all their cantering work, I keep fit enough for competition. However, if you are riding only one horse, it is a good idea to do some other form of exercise.

Skipping and cycling are two very good exercises for riding, as they help strengthen the legs. You will also need to do exercises to strengthen the back and stomach muscles, and the arms. If you live near a gymnasium or fitness centre, it is worth consulting one of the trained staff there to help you work out a programme tailored to your particular sport.

When I am galloping or cantering the horses I ride quite a lot shorter than I do normally for cross-country. It is a good idea to get used to riding shorter, as this uses different muscles and also helps to improve your balance. It is important to train yourself to ride in a more balanced way, even if you are one of those lucky people who is naturally well balanced.

Riding technique

It is very important, particularly when you are doing flat work, that you have regular instruction, or at least some help from someone knowledge-able on the ground. If you have no one to keep an eye on you, it is all too easy to slip into bad habits without realising it. Once you have acquired a bad habit, it is difficult to eradicate it. Also, someone on the ground can often see something that you cannot feel, or can suggest the answer to a problem more easily than you.

Skipping is a very good exercise for those riders who find they need to do extra training to get themselves fit.

Rider psychology

You need to prepare yourself mentally as well as physically for an event. The most important thing is to try to keep yourself relaxed. You are bound to get a bit excited and tense before a competition, even a one-day event. Recently there has been a great deal written about sports psychology – getting yourself into the right frame of mind for a contest. Basically, experience teaches you how to behave under competition conditions. I am lucky in that I am a fairly relaxed sort of person anyway, so I do not have to do anything to psyche myself up for an event. The biggest mistake for me is to start thinking about winning. If I get too absorbed in winning it affects my performance.

It can help the novice rider to remember that, initially, he is just out to enjoy himself; there is no need to get wound up about the competition. The object is to educate your horse and to have fun, and there is no point in becoming too competitive early on as you will not do your horse or yourself any good. The main thing is to stay relaxed. If you can remain calm, your mind will be able to absorb what is going on around you and you will be able to react in the right way to any problems that may occur.

Your preparations at home can have a great influence on your mental approach to an event. If you are happy that you have done your homework, and have trained the horse to the best of his ability and to the level required for that particular event, then you can go into the competition feeling reasonably confident. I think that this is very important. If you have had hiccups in the training and you are not sure whether the horse is capable of coping with the level of competition you have entered, it is very easy to become negative, and that affects your performance. Once you arrive at a competition any lingering worries must be put firmly to the back of your mind, and from then on you must assume a positive attitude to the job in hand, be it the dressage, the cross-country or the show jumping. If you allow yourself to entertain negative thoughts then you might as well leave the horse in the stable, because you will not put up a good performance.

I have a lucky pair of socks, which sounds pretty silly, but something like that can help your mental attitude towards the competition. If you happen to believe that the particular pair of socks you are wearing is lucky, then you are going to feel happier. It all boils down to positive thinking.

I find that I get nervous because I want to do well, not because I am frightened. Nerves are a good thing, as long as you can control them and don't allow them to get the better of you. They must be positive nerves. If you find yourself getting into a state before a competition then you have just got to take a hold of yourself, sit down and think about what you are doing and put the whole thing into perspective. Some people get into a complete stew before a competition, and go to pieces. It is all to do with mind control, and different people find different ways of coping with it. Some riders actually need to work up a bit of a frenzy before they can compete well, but I know that I need to be in a very relaxed state. These days I do not really have to work at it. I know I can quickly put myself in the right frame of mind to do as well as possible.

The ten-minute halt at the start of the cross-country is probably the most nerve-racking time, though it always seems to pass very quickly. I used to find time to indulge in a cigarette, but now that I have given up smoking, I can't do that! By the time you have seen to your horse, gone to the loo, watched the TV monitor (if there is one), and caught up with the news, it is time to go. I like to talk to other people to find out what has been happening on the course, but you have to be careful what you take in. It is very easy to be given the wrong advice at this crucial stage.

If you are going to receive advice, make sure that it comes from someone who knows you and your horse very well, otherwise it may be irrelevant. Jumping a fence in a particular way might suit one horse but not suit yours, and the person advising you needs to know that. I tend to take in only what I want to know. Nowadays if I hear that a particular fence has been causing problems it does not put me off, in fact I usually want to know who has fallen, where they have fallen, and why. In some ways that can make me even more determined to go clear. But for the first-timer that sort of information may be disheartening.

I remember the first time that I competed at Badminton, in 1980, when I won on Southern Comfort. By the time I set out on the cross-country there was only one horse who had gone clear within the time. Horses had been falling and getting eliminated all over the place. A friend of mine, Sally O'Connor, was in the box, but she did not tell me about this, so I was oblivious to the carnage that had gone on ahead of me. I went out thinking that everyone was getting round, so I had better get round too. If I had known at that stage, fairly early in my career, that most people had been crashing, I am not sure how I would have reacted.

Try to ensure that your adviser knows you well enough to give you the sort of information that will make you feel happy about your ride. Nevertheless, if a particular fence is causing serious trouble, it is always better to know about it so that you can take an alternative route or change your plan accordingly.

CHAPTER 6

Equipment for Horse and Rider

Safety is the main consideration when it comes to equipment for the speed and endurance. The last thing you want is an accident resulting from a piece of broken saddlery; and the rider should always be well protected, whatever the level of competition. At the beginning of the season and two weeks before a big event carefully check your saddlery for any loose stitching or weak leather, so that you can have it repaired if necessary. Always take spare leathers, reins, girths, etc. with you to an event.

The horse's equipment
Bits

You need to be flexible about the type of bit you use on a horse, and be prepared to experiment. Unfortunately, you will not always get the same feel from a new bit at home, where your horse will be more relaxed, as you will at an event, where most horses react differently. I can get away with cantering Michaelmas Day in an ordinary snaffle at home, but at a competition I would find myself in real strife with the same bit. I normally put him in a pelham for the speed and endurance.

Vulcanite pelham with roundings (rein couplings) and a rubber chain guard. This is one of my favourite bits for a very strong horse.

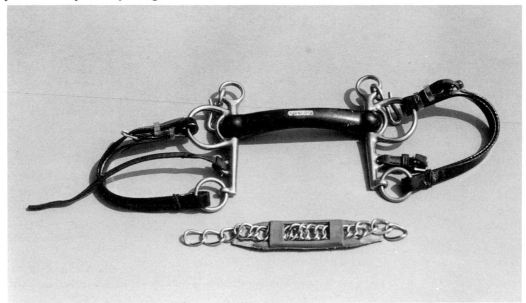

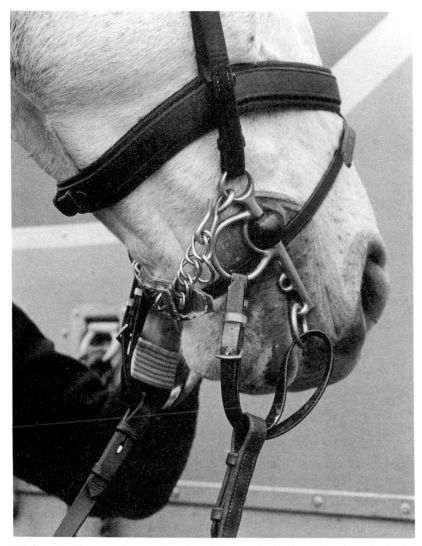

Welton Greylag wearing a vulcanite pelham and a flash noseband, ready for the cross-country.

If you find a bit in which your horse is happy and goes well, then that is fine, but if he starts to become too strong in it you may need to think again. It is sometimes worth trying a softer bit, as horses do not always go better in a stronger bit. There are no hard-and-fast rules; you simply have to experiment. Unfortunately the only way to give a new bit a real test is to try it out in a competition, and if you've made the wrong choice you could be in trouble.

Careful schooling will certainly improve the way a horse goes and make him less resistant in the mouth, but some horses are born stronger in the jaw than others, so you must be prepared to try different bits.

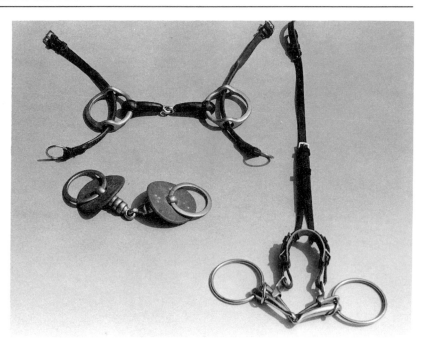

Top left: *Rubber gag. I used this bit on Peppermint Park, a horse who galloped with his head very low. It is quite effective on horses who are difficult to pick up in front of a fence.* Bottom left: *Roller snaffle. I used this on Felix Too, who was fairly strong. This was a bit that he was comfortable in and it also gave me enough control.* Right: *Citation bit. This bit is used more extensively in racing for very hard-pulling horses. It has a very severe action.*

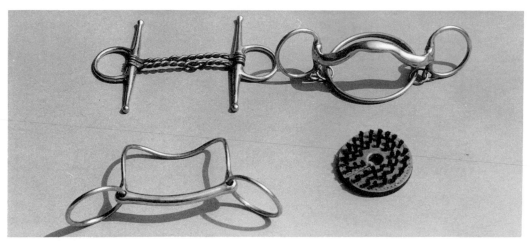

Top left: *Double-twisted copper wire bit with cheekpieces – a severe bit.* Bottom left: *New Zealand hanging bit. This is an excellent bit for horses who do not turn easily, as it puts pressure on the bottom jaw when turning. It is often seen in racing.* Bottom right: *This brush fits over the mouthpiece, between the horse's face and the bit ring. It is used to help turn a horse. My wife, Carolyn, uses one on Done For Fun.* Top right: *German correction bit with hanging ring. This bit has a high port to stop the horse getting his tongue over the bit, and the ring helps to turn the horse.*

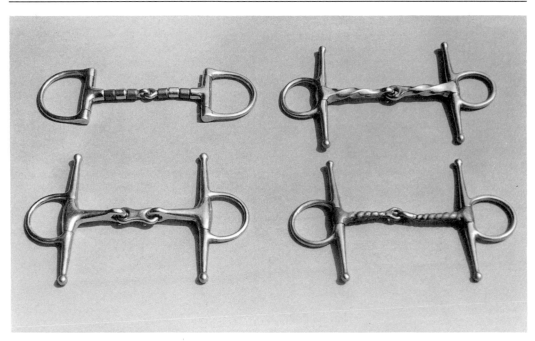

All these bits are slightly sharper than a normal snaffle. Top left: *Copper roller snaffle.* Bottom left: *Eggbutt snaffle with French link and cheekpieces.* Bottom right: *Jointed copper corkscrew (twisted snaffle) bit with cheekpieces.* Top right: *Cheeked jointed snaffle with a soft twist.*

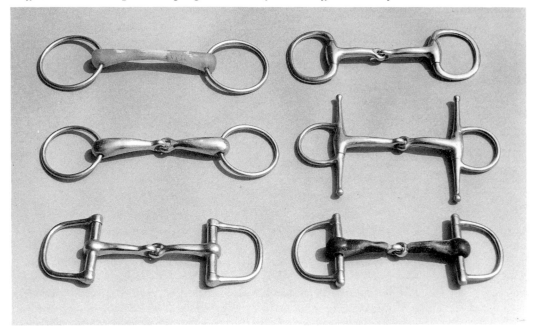

Variations on the plain snaffle. Left, top to bottom: *Nylon straight bar snaffle: loose-ring jointed snaffle; D-ring snaffle.* Right, top to bottom: *plain eggbutt jointed snaffle; eggbutt jointed snaffle with cheekpieces; vulcanite D-ring jointed snaffle.*

Nosebands

I generally like to use a grakle or flash noseband for cross-country because they work both on the jaw and the nose and they keep the horse's mouth shut, which is important if your horse tries to evade the bit by opening his mouth. Some horses are so soft and light in the mouth that they go well in a cavesson.

Reins

My preference is for rubber reins. My hands are quite large so I like fairly wide reins so that I can get a good grip on them. I am not so keen on the web reins with leather grips because when you have to slip the reins it is more difficult to let them slide through your fingers.

Before the cross-country, some people like to put insulation tape around the billets of their reins for extra security. This is something I have never done because I feel that if you have checked your equipment thoroughly and it is in good condition, then it should not be necessary.

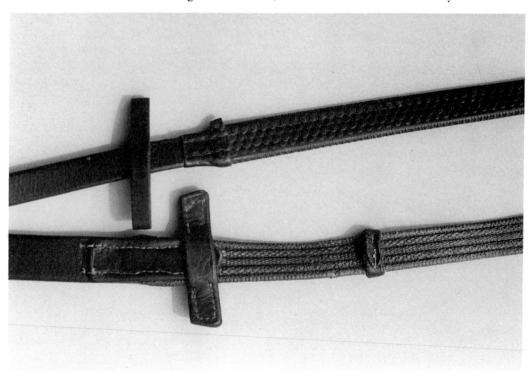

Top: *Rubber reins.* Bottom: *Web reins with leather grips. Both reins have martingale stoppers on them.*

Martingales

I very seldom school in a martingale. If a horse is educated properly from the beginning he should not need one. However, I normally put on a martingale, quite loosely, for the speed and endurance at a competition, just in case the horse does put his head up for some reason.

Saddles

Any forward-seat saddle is suitable as long as it fits well. Make sure that it does not sit down on the horse's wither when you tighten up the

Some of the cross-country saddles that I have used in the last ten years. Most of them are fairly lightweight and forward-cut. The saddle in the foreground is the one I favour at present because it has a fairly flat seat to allow me to get my weight well back if necessary. I do not like saddles that have big knee rolls or thigh pads, like the one on the left, because I find that the rolls tend to push my leg out of position.

overgirth. Its shape is really a question of what you find most comfortable. Personally, I do not like saddles with big knee rolls because these tend to push my leg out of position more often than they help to keep it in place. I always use a numnah, usually one of the artificial sheepskin variety, to provide a cushion between the saddle and the horse's back.

Girths

A girth with an elastic gusset helps to allow the horse to expand his rib cage when he is galloping. This applies equally to the overgirth, which goes right over the top of the saddle. You should always fit an overgirth in case your normal girth breaks. I usually use a lightweight nylon one as this helps to keep my overall weight down. For the same reason, I also use lightweight aluminium irons.

Breastplate

This is essential to keep the saddle in position. I like to use one with a martingale attachment.

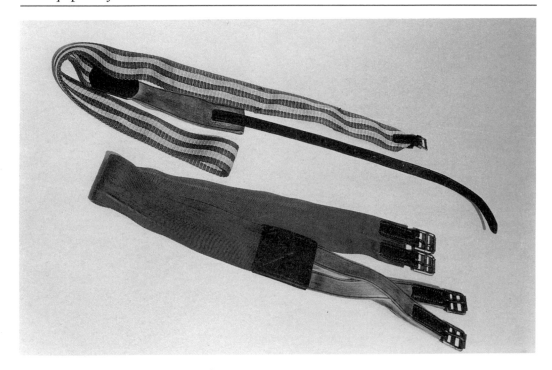

The type of surcingle (top) and girth that I use for the cross-country. Both are made of lightweight nylon, which helps to keep my total weight down. I like them to be elasticated, to allow more freedom for the horse. The stitching and elastic should be checked regularly for signs of wear and tear.

Weight cloth

In a three-day event or an advanced one-day event the minimum weight you have to carry is 11 stone 11lb (75kg). This can include your saddle and, if necessary, your bridle. I am over 11 stone 11lb (75kg) even without the saddle, so for three-day events I try to get my weight down as much as possible.

If you have to carry lead, it is good idea to work your horse with the weight cloth occasionally so that he gets accustomed to carrying the dead weight. It is best to do this when you are hacking or schooling the horse. There is no point in making him carry the weight for fast work; this just puts unnecessary strain on the horse's legs.

The weight cloth that my wife, Carolyn, uses has pockets for the lead in front of and behind the saddle. Approximately two thirds of the weight should be borne in the front and the rest behind, as it is easier for the horse to carry the weight across his shoulders than in the middle of his back. It is important that you distribute the weight evenly on either side of the horse. Carolyn has to carry about 2 stone (12½kg) in lead, so her weight cloth has hooks that hold it up into the gullet of the saddle, and this keeps the weight off the horse's spine.

At an advanced one-day event you are weighed only at the finish, but at a three-day event you are weighed at the start of Phase A and then again at the end of Phase D. It is a good idea, particularly if it is hot, to carry a few

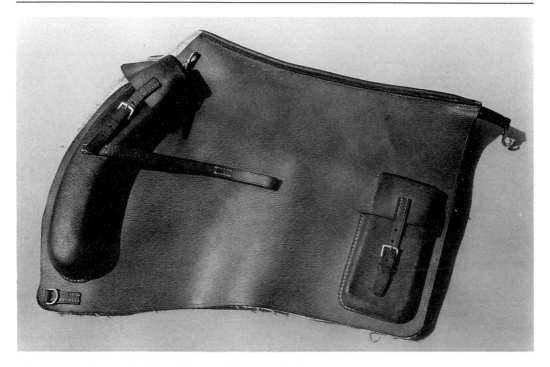

This is a good type of weight cloth as it distributes lead both in front of and behind the saddle. The weight cloth is attached to the saddle by specially designed clips, which prevent it from sitting on the horse's spine.

pounds over the minimum weight, because over the whole endurance day you may lose several pounds of your own body weight. If you are right on the borderline to start with, you may find you are a bit underweight at the end of the cross-country. You can throw in your bridle to add an extra 2lb (1kg), but if you are still underweight after that you will be eliminated.

Studs

You will need different types of studs for different conditions. If the ground is hard I use small studs, and if it is very wet, much bigger ones are needed. On sandy going you do not usually need any studs at all.

Boots and bandages

I hardly ever use exercise bandages. As already stated, there is so much pressure on a horse's legs when he is cantering and galloping that I do not think bandages are going to make a lot of difference. Unless you are very good at putting on bandages you can cause uneven pressure on the legs, particularly if the bandages get wet, and then they will do more harm than good.

In competition all my horses wear leather protector boots with a soft, rubber lining. They are fastened with buckles, over which I usually apply tape as an extra precaution against them coming undone. These boots offer very good protection, are easy to put on and do not slip.

There are several different kinds of overreach boot available. I prefer to

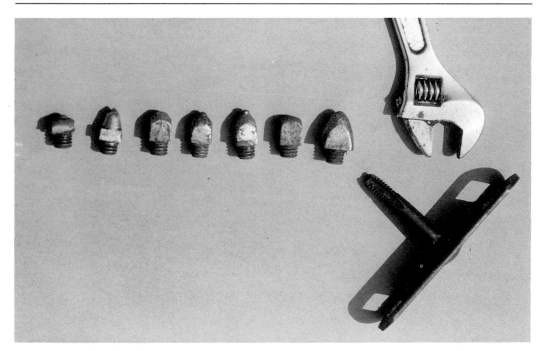

Various types of stud with spanner and T-shaped thread cleaner. The smaller and sharper studs are used on hard ground; the larger, squarer ones are used on soft ground.

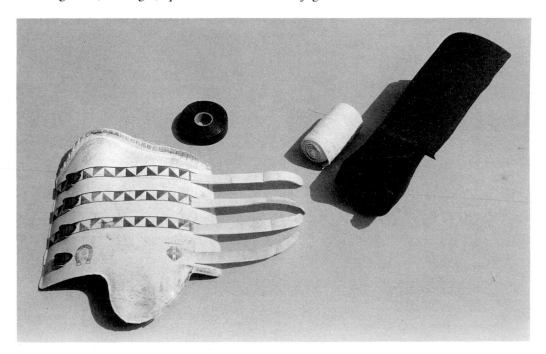

Left: *Hind leg boot, with tape to secure the straps once they have been buckled.* Right: *Front leg protector, which is secured by a bandage.*

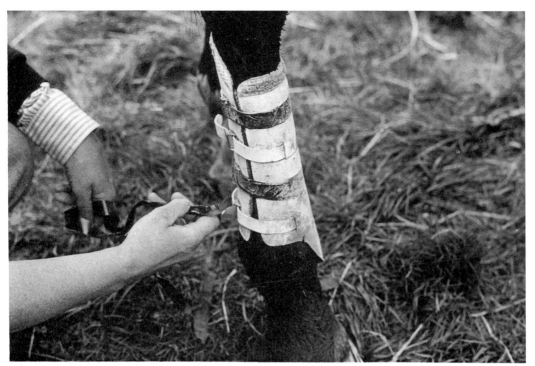

Hind leg boot with the straps being taped. This is an extra precaution to make sure that the boots stay in place.

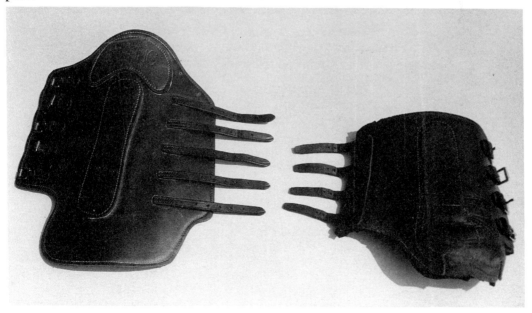

Front and rear boots made of leather, which I prefer. The rear boots (left) protect high up the inside of the leg and also the inside of the fetlock. The front ones (right) come right down the back of the fetlock joint and they protect the tendon.

use fairly short ones so that there is less chance of the horse treading on the back of the boot with a hind foot, and so tripping himself up.

The only time I use stable bandages is in the last two or three weeks before a major competition – unless, of course, there is a specific problem that requires bandaging. I do not think that it is very healthy for horses to be bandaged all the time, and some individuals can become so reliant on bandages worn in the stable that as soon as you take them off their legs fill anyway. I prefer to see what the horse's legs are like, and to see if there are any changes. If a horse's legs do tend to swell in the stable, it is better to find the reason than to rely on bandages. Ask yourself what you have done in the last twenty-four hours that may have caused the horse's legs to fill. Perhaps you have over-extended him, or changed his diet.

If this happens during the last fortnight before a big competition then it is worth bandaging. I tend to do it anyway out of habit. It guards against knocks in the stable; it offers support to the legs, and it also keeps the legs · warmer and stimulates circulation.

If you are bandaging your horse for a long journey you must be very careful. I have seen horses who have been left for twenty-four hours with badly bandaged legs coming off a plane with bowed tendons. You need to use very thick wraps underneath the bandages to help even out the pressure. There are now several very good types of wraps made specifically for use under stable or travelling bandages. If you do not have suitable wraps you are better off just putting protective boots on the horse.

For long-distance travelling I prefer to use a tail guard rather than a tail bandage. If the bandage is put on too tightly you can cut off the circulation in the tail.

Rugs

You will need to take a good selection of rugs to an event. If it rains, you will need a waterproof rug to keep the horse dry before you go cross-country; if it is hot, you will need a sweat sheet. If you are travelling a long distance you should be prepared for extremes in temperature. You might start off your journey on a hot day, but by the night it may be very cold. Try to keep as much air as possible circulating in the lorry so that the horses do not get stuffy.

For a one-day event I usually take the following rugs:

1 cotton sheet
1 wool rug
1 sweat sheet
1 waterproof rug

For a three-day event the horse's night rugs will be needed as well. It may also pay to take spares in case some of the day rugs get wet.

The rider's equipment

For safety, you must wear an approved crash helmet with the harness correctly fitted. (If your chin strap comes undone while you are competing on the cross-country you risk elimination.) You must also wear a back protector, which you strap on to your back under your shirt or sweater. There are a number of different varieties on the market.

A lightweight, woollen, American-style cooler rug. This is particularly useful on cold days for drying off a horse after the cross-country.

It is also a good idea to wear a long-sleeved shirt, however hot it is, so that your arms are protected. Similarly, gloves protect the hands, and can have a non-slip action when the reins become wet from your horse's sweat or from an untimely downpour. For this reason, leather gloves are not much use unless you have rubber reins. String and 'pimple' gloves are usually more effective. Personally I like to wear fingerless gloves, as I find that these give my hands and fingers more flexibility when I am riding across country.

Stocks or hunting ties should be worn across country. These are believed to give support to the neck and reduce the risk of injury, though I think their effectiveness is doubtful. It is very important to remove the stock pin before you set off across country because if you do have a fall the pin could cause a serious injury.

I always wear spurs and carry a whip when riding cross-country. You never know when you might need to give your horse a reminder to get you out of trouble. The blunt-ended type of spur must be used, and if the shank is curved, the spurs should be worn with the shank pointing

Above left: *One of the wide variety of back protectors available. It is compulsory to wear one when riding cross-country at a BHS event.*

Above right: *Another type of back protector. Most of these are now available with shoulder pads for extra protection. The rider is wearing a stock, from which the stock pin has been removed as it could cause a serious injury in the event of a fall.*

Right: *I like to use fingerless gloves for riding across country.*

Some of the different types of spurs that are allowed at BHS events.

downwards. Whips for cross-country must not exceed 30 inches (76.2cm) in length. If you have any doubts about the equipment you plan to use, you should consult your rule book.

CHAPTER 7 *Competitions*

Planning your season

There is nothing like competition experience to bring a horse on, but this does not mean that you should run your horse at every available event. You need a goal to aim for – whether it be to upgrade your horse or to compete in a novice three-day event, for example – then you can plan your campaign accordingly to give your horse the best possible preparation. This may mean running him for three weekends in a row, and then giving him a break from competition for a couple of weeks, or it may mean taking him out two or three times over a period of six weeks. Only experience will tell. I have found that if I take a novice horse to two or three events in quick succession he will learn very quickly from each one and come on a great deal – but he will need a short break afterwards.

With a youngster starting out as a novice you should be very careful to avoid hard and rough ground. I like to give a novice five or six starts in the spring, and then, once the ground begins to harden, put him away for a couple of months. Then I bring him back in the autumn and compete in a few more events. You should not run a young horse into the ground. An older novice horse – an eight-, nine- or ten-year-old – will be able to withstand more work than an immature five- or six-year-old.

The number of events I do with an older and more experienced horse will depend very much on the horse and on what I am aiming him for. An advanced horse preparing for a three-day event will probably do two or three one-day competitions beforehand to help build up his fitness and to sharpen up his jumping in a competition atmosphere.

One thing is certain: you do your horse no good at all if you run him flat out every weekend. He might endure this punishment for a while, but you will be clocking up senseless wear and tear and, unless your horse has legs of iron, it is going to catch up with him eventually.

Speed is the thing that causes the most damage to your horse. If you are going out mostly for experience and you maintain a steady pace on the cross-country, then you will not take a lot out of a horse and you can afford to run him more often. It depends to a certain extent on what sort of rider you are and how experienced your horse is. Some riders are so competitive that they find it very difficult not to go fast every time they ride at an event. I used to try to win every time I went out, but now, especially with a novice horse, I will have a go only if the horse is ready for it and if he is in a good position after the dressage and show jumping. If I am lying twenty-third after the dressage, for example, I would not go flat out in the hope of moving up to ninth place.

Your first competition

Before going to your first event make sure that you have studied the rule book carefully, so that, particularly on the cross-country phase, you understand the flagging, the scoring system, the timing and so on. Check that you have the correct equipment for yourself and your horse. A back protector and an approved skull cap are now compulsory for the cross-country.

Make sure, also, that you know when to ring up the competition secretary to find out your starting times in all three phases of the one-day event. This is normally the evening before the competition. If it is a local event, you may wish to walk the course the afternoon before the competition. If not, then you will be able to tell from the times you are given whether you have sufficient time to walk the course between the dressage and show jumping, or between the show jumping and the cross-country. Otherwise you will need to allow enough time to walk the course before you warm up for your dressage. A novice cross-country course will usually take between forty minutes and an hour to walk thoroughly.

Walking a cross-country course is discussed in more detail in the next chapter, but at a novice event the courses are usually quite straightforward so the most important thing is to learn the route. There will be a plan of the course in the schedule, which you can collect, along with your number, from the secretary's tent when you arrive at the event. You should carry this plan with you when you walk the course, checking the number of each fence as you go by. It is very easy, if you are not concentrating, to miss out a fence that is tucked away from the main route, perhaps in a wood. Also, some events run intermediate and novice courses over parts of the same track, so you will need to make sure that you do not confuse your obstacles with those of the intermediate section. If any of the fences have alternatives, study these thoroughly so that you know which will suit your horse best, and where you are least likely to have a problem.

Some people, even at novice level, like to walk a course more than once. If you find after your first walk that you still do not know your exact route then it would certainly pay you to walk the course a second time. You cannot afford to be dithering, wondering where you are supposed to be going, when you should be concentrating on riding the next fence. If you are concerned about any particular fences, you may have time to watch other competitors jumping them to see how they ride. You will also need to decide whether or not you want your horse to wear studs. At novice level on good, dry going I rarely use them. However, if the going is wet or the ground a little slippery then I fit studs according to the conditions.

You will probably need to ride in two or three events before you know how your horse is going to react at a competition, and therefore how long he will need to warm up for the dressage. With young horses I do not like to do much more than half an hour, because it is very difficult to keep their concentration for any longer and they become tired quite quickly. I find that if a horse gets used to having a long warm up he may become dependent on it, then you always have to do it. If I am competing on three or four novice horses in a day, I have to give them a very quick warm-up because my schedule is so tight, but I find that they usually adapt to this and go just as well.

You will also need to consider how best your horse's feeds can be fitted in around his competition times. During the day I like a horse to be fed at his normal times if possible, but I never give a horse a feed less than two hours before he is due to compete in any of the tests at a one-day event.

If your show jumping is, say, about an hour after your dressage this should give you enough time to return to your lorry, change whatever tack is necessary and ride back to the show-jumping arena. A twenty-minute warm-up is probably all that is necessary at this level of competition because the horse has already been ridden-in on the flat. After a little trot and canter work to loosen up the horse again, you can start your jumping preparation. If, however, you ride your dressage test early in the morning and your show jumping is not until the afternoon, you will need to spend more time on the flat before you start jumping, to make sure that the horse is listening to the leg and hand and is going forward. You should not need to do a lot of jumping preparation. Just pop the horse over an upright and an oxer until he is clearing them confidently, and as long as you are happy with the way he is jumping he should be ready to go into the arena. At this stage there is no point in trying to school him or in having a battle with him over jumping technique.

Lucinda Green adjusting her saddle. The horse is wearing a screen to protect him from the flies. Lucinda is correctly dressed for cross-country riding, and is wearing a back protector.

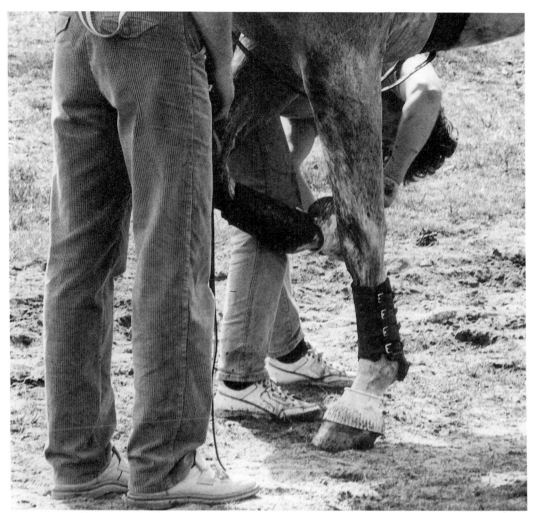

Checking the studs before setting off across country. The photograph also shows the front boots and overreach boots correctly fitted.

The same applies to the cross-country. If it comes shortly after your show jumping you will not need a lengthy warm-up; but if you have waited several hours between these two tests you will have to prepare more thoroughly. This may entail trot work for five minutes, followed by some steady cantering, and then asking the horse to gallop on to let him know that it is time for him to gear himself up for the cross-country. Make sure that your horse is thinking forward over the practice fence. If he is not concentrating or is hanging back and not taking you to the fence then wake him up, using your stick if necessary, to get him going. Don't wait until you set off on the cross-country to do this, or you may find that you have a stop at the first fence.

No matter how much schooling you have done in preparation for your

Stable bandages. I like to have good, thick wraps under the bandages which help to even out the pressure of the bandage on a horse's legs, and, if you have to bandage a horse continuously the wraps help to prevent crinkles on the horse's skin. These are long bandages which enable you to wrap the horse's leg from below the fetlock to just below the knee.

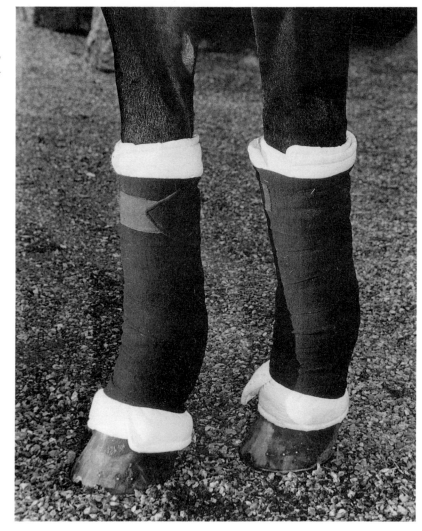

first event, a young horse is always liable to act slightly differently in his early competitions. For his first few events, I do not worry about a horse's cross-country speed at all, as long as I can make him go forward, between hand and leg, at a controlled pace. Obviously if the horse is a bit of a tearaway, then you need to control that speed early on so that he learns to settle and to go at the pace you want. As the horse gains more confidence, you can gradually increase the pace and the rhythm until, eventually, your horse can complete a novice course within the optimum time without ever having to be hurried.

Avoid pushing a horse fast too early as you may frighten him. You should not try to gallop flat out between the fences and then hook back to jump each fence. This teaches a horse to rush and pull, and it is a much more tiring way of riding a course. *Always aim to keep a constant rhythm.*

After the cross-country I usually walk the horse straight back to the lorry and then take off all the tack, including the boots, and quickly check for any signs of injury. If it is cold the horse will be sponged off around his head, neck and saddle regions, then covered with a rug so that he does not get chilled; on a warmer day the horse can be washed off completely and the excess water scraped off, and then a sweat sheet put on. He should then be walked round until he has stopped blowing and has completely dried off. Once he is dry he is allowed a small drink, and at this time you can attend to any small nicks or grazes that he may have.

If the going has been good, I dry-wrap a novice horse's legs; but if I have been competing on hard ground I use 'Ice-Tight', or some form of poultice that is fairly easy to apply, to help draw out of the horse's legs any heat or swelling. These wraps are put on once the horse has cooled down. An hour or so after the horse has completely dried off from the cross-country he can have another drink and a small haynet to pick at, and he is then ready to travel home. If you have used studs, do not forget to take them out before you go.

CHAPTER 8   *Walking the Course*

Walking a course correctly is one of the most important pre-requisites to achieving a good cross-country ride. The main objective is to familiarise yourself with the route and with the obstacles that you are going to jump, so that you can decide how you are going to ride them, and exactly where you are going to jump each fence. You will also need to assess the going, the type of terrain and any other factors that may influence your approach to the course.

The number of times that you need to walk a course depends on how good you are at memorising the fences. At a one-day event I normally walk the course only once, because after years of practice I find that I am able quickly to make a mental note of each fence and where I want to jump it. If it is not possible to walk the course in advance, you will need to arrive at the competition with sufficient time in hand to walk it before you start warming up for the dressage.

If possible, aim to walk the course at approximately the same time of day as you are going to be riding it, because the position of the sun can have a dramatic effect on some fences. (This is not usually possible at a one-day event unless you walk the course the day before, but you can plan to do this at a three-day event.) You might, for example, walk the course when the sun is behind you as you approach a particular fence, but when you come to ride it the sun could be glaring in your face and distract your horse. You also need to pay special attention to fences where you will be jumping from bright sunshine into relative darkness (e.g. into a wood), as this can be off-putting to a horse.

When you are walking a course pay attention to the terrain, the type of fences, and the direction of your approach to each fence. These will all affect the way in which you tackle a particular obstacle. For example, the ground may slope downwards into a fence, or you may have an uphill approach; you may have to avoid some rough or uneven ground in front of a fence or on the landing side. Each fence and the problems it poses will determine, to a certain extent, the speed at which you ride it. You must also consider the direction of your approach, and, if a turn is necessary, work out exactly where you need to make that turn to get yourself in line for the fence.

At combinations you will have to decide exactly where you are going to take each element, and where you are heading, so that you can line up the fences in your mind's eye. Remember that with a young horse you will need to give yourself plenty of room to get the line straight. Where

Measuring the distance at the White Label Water Garden at Badminton, where there was a bounce into water over a brush fence. The two fences were at a slight angle to each other; on the left the distance was shorter than on the right. I opted for the middle where the distance was about 12ft – 12ft 6ins (3.6 –3.75m). The horses could not see the water until they had virtually taken off over the second brush. As you landed over the first brush, you had to be ready to be strong with the leg, so that when your horse did see the water you were in a position to push him on.

Looking over the top of fence 6 at Badminton, 1990. This was a fairly straightforward obstacle, but you had to jump it on a slight angle to the left because the railings beside the road (to the right of the picture) curved in towards the obstacle. You could not see the landing from where you took off, and there was a sizeable ditch, of which you needed to be aware. The further left you jumped the fence, the bigger the ditch was, and the further right you jumped it, the quicker you had to turn because you were running into the rails beside the road.

alternatives exist, always take time to study all the possible routes, so that if you have to change your plan at the last minute you will know exactly where to go.

When you are assessing combinations there are usually several factors to weigh up. Normally the most direct route is the most difficult, the other route or routes varying in their degree of difficulty and differing in the length of time needed to negotiate them. Bearing in mind the horse you are riding, you have to decide which is the quickest route that you can safely take through that obstacle. To ride fast across country you sometimes have to take a bit of a risk, but it should never be a dangerous risk. A few time penalties are preferable to 20 penalties for a stop, or 60 penalties for a fall. If I am in any doubt about my horse's capabilities of doing the fast route, I will always take the slightly longer, safer option.

At a three-day event there is normally an official course walk the day before the competition starts. Competitors are driven round the first phase of the roads and tracks, then they walk the steeplechase, and then are driven round the remainder of the roads and tracks. It may only be necessary to do this once, depending on the complexity of the route, but if you are in any doubt it is worth asking for a second drive-round. You may also feel the need to walk the steeplechase a second time, making sure that you know where the half-way or the minute markers are on the course. Most international three-day event steeplechase courses are laid out in a figure-of-eight, but some are ridden as two circuits in the same direction.

Walking the steeplechase course. The prime objective is to get a feel for the fences and the state of the ground, and to familiarise yourself with the direction you are going, particularly on a figure-of-eight course, which can be more confusing. It also pays to know if any open ditches appear on the course, or if there is any variation in the type of fence.

Seoul Olympics, 1988. The approach to this combination was downhill, and the ground was falling away to the left. The most direct route was to jump the first element on the second panel from the left, then one long stride and jump the corner. The quickest of the alternative routes was again to jump the second panel from the left, but this time on a left-to-right angle so that you took one stride to the middle of the second element, then you made a sharp turn back to jump the three rails of the third element.

Riding Charisma, I chose the quick alternative because the only times he had ever run out on corners were at those where he could duck out to the left. Because you had to commit yourself to this corner off a long stride, which meant that you had less control, I decided there was too much risk involved in having a run-out at this fence, so I played for the safer option. Charisma was such a fast horse that I knew we could make up the time elsewhere.

Here riders had the option of negotiating a ditch and rail or jumping the whole thing in one. Normally, if there is a choice between one jumping effort as opposed to two or three, I will take the one effort as it is less tiring on the horse. Big ditches, like the one here which has rails going right to the bottom of the ditch, create an optical illusion of a huge fence. Whilst this can intimidate the rider, the horse will not always see it that way. If your horse has been well schooled over ditches from the beginning he should not have a problem with a fence like this and you need not worry about how big it looks. This type of fence usually jumps very well.

Plenty to think about here – the Osuna Brand, an obstacle on the cross-country at the 1984 Los Angeles Olympics. The fence came about threequarters of the way round the course and was approached from the left of the picture. The most favoured option was to jump the left-hand part of the fence, go straight on and jump the curve of the J, turn and come back over the nearside (i.e. leaving the picture in the bottom left-hand corner). I was one of only two riders who took the short option: over the second panel from the left of the first element, then three strides on a right-hand curve to jump the stem of the J, followed by another three strides to jump the third panel from the left of the last element. This involved jumping three sets of parallel rails on a fairly tight semi-circle, which needed considerable skill and honesty on the horse's part, but the route saved five or six seconds. So I took a calculated risk with Charisma, who was a very nippy, neat jumping horse, and he did it very well.

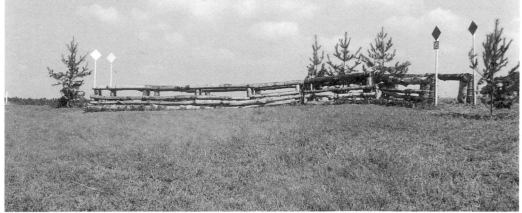

This fence probably caused more problems than any other on the course in Seoul, although it looked the most harmless. A fairly low, wide oxer was perched on an uphill incline, so you were not aware of the width of the obstacle until you were upon it. A lot of horses came up the hill and jumped into the middle of the oxer because they appeared not to have seen the back rail. You had to ride the fence very strongly, but not too fast, to make sure that your horse jumped right out over it. Low, wide obstacles are often the most difficult for a horse to jump because there is not sufficient height to get them into the air to manage the spread. You have to use your own strength to tell the horse what to expect.

This fence caused quite a few worries when we walked the course in Seoul. It had a very long, steep approach to the rails on top of the hill then, as you jumped the obstacle, the ground immediately fell away on the other side. You had to attack the hill strongly enough to make the horse jump the fence, but at the same time you risked over-jumping it, which is what a couple of horses did, landing about 20ft (7m) away down the other side. You have to be careful at a fence like this where a horse cannot see where he will land.

I was not too worried about it with Charisma because he had become very careful in his old age and he was so experienced that he knew exactly what was happening. He galloped up to it, popped over the rails at the top of the hill, landed on the ground just the other side and galloped away again.

When you are driving round the roads and tracks keep an eye on the terrain, so that you will know if there are any rough or stoney sections and you can choose the best ground to ride on. Look out also for the kilometre markers, and make a note of the compulsory check points. The latter are marked by red and white flags, which you have to pass through. At the competitors' briefing you are normally given a map showing the route for the roads and tracks and pointing out all the compulsory check points.

Most people walk a three-day event cross-country course three or four times. I like to walk it as many times as are necessary for me to know exactly where I am going to jump each fence. At a major three-day event this is usually four times. The first look, on the official walk, is normally just to familiarise yourself with each fence, and to get a feel of the terrain and the area that you are going to be riding around. As you approach each fence on this first walk it is worth remembering that this is how they will appear to your horse. Although *you* will know exactly what each fence

The Waterfalls (Los Angeles, 1984). This was an unusual fence because you had to jump over two waterfalls. The water was not particularly deep and the obstacle was fairly well on in the course, by which stage most horses, if they are going at all well, will keep going. Although people were worried about the waterfalls, they jumped very well, and the biggest problem was the left turn into the last element out of the water (fence 23). Here the water was quite deep, and some horses made untidy jumps getting out. A lot of horses trotted through the water, which was fine.

At this sort of fence it is important to check the depth of the water and the surface underneath it when you walk the course. This will mean taking off your shoes and getting into the water to walk the line that you plan to ride with your horse. You also want to be aware of where the sun will be and whether there might be any reflections in front or behind the obstacles which could be off-putting to the horse.

entails by the time you come to ride the cross-country, your horse will not, and he may not always realise what is expected of him.

I do not pay too much attention to detail on the first walk. I take a general look at all the options and take in the course as a whole. It is on the second walk round, which I do on the first day of dressage, that I study each fence in depth, looking closely at all the options, studying carefully all the lines for each fence. This can take a long time so there is no point being in a hurry.

On this course walk I also check the going between the fences to see if there are any patches of rough or wet ground, so that I can choose the best, most economical line to take between each fence. I also look out for any bad ground in front of or behind a fence. At this stage I find it useful to walk the course with someone else, to get their views on the fences. Sometimes another person sees things differently and has conflicting ideas. These may not necessarily suit your horse or the way you want to ride a

Seoul Olympics, 1988 – the first water obstacle. There were two sets of upright rails going into the water with a related distance, so it was important to jump the first element well to get your striding right for the second. When you walked the course you had to work out exactly how many strides you wanted to get in and at what pace you would have to approach on your particular horse to achieve that number of strides accurately, so that you could be in the best possible position to jump the fence into the water.

Checking the footing and depth of water. Here, at the obstacle out of the water in Seoul, there was a bank up, but it was bigger and more clearly defined than the one in Los Angeles (see next picture), so the horses were less likely to trip up it. This was followed by a steep uphill pull to another set of rails, which required the rider to take immediate action to get his horse in the correct place to jump the rails.

The Bridge and Walkway (Los Angeles). With a fence that has a small ledge coming out of water you need to be sure that you get a clean jump up on to the bank. Otherwise your horse is likely to leave a back leg behind or paddle up with his front legs, and then it becomes virtually impossible for him to jump whatever comes next, particularly if it is a bounce. If the obstacle into the water is fairly close to the bank out (one long stride in this case) you need to ride for that stride. If you have a long pull through water, it is better to keep going and wait until you see your stride to a good spot on the bank. If the horse comes back to a trot, you are usually better off staying in trot, but keep plenty of impulsion.

fence, but at least you have a different opinion on it.

It is also a good opportunity to measure the course, so that you can work out your timing. You will need to borrow a measuring wheel for this, or walk with someone who has one. You can then calculate where you should be at what time. The way I do this is to make a note of where each minute marker is. If, for example, the speed of the cross-country is 570 m per minute, I measure every 570 metres with the wheel, and then try to pick out a good reference point to remind me of where that minute marker is. When riding the course I do not look at my watch every minute that goes by, but if I have measured all the markers in advance I can choose three or four that come up at times when it is convenient to look at my watch.

When you measure the course, walk the most direct route, as that is normally the way it is measured by the course designer. Check to see that your measurement agrees with the length given on the course plan. If yours is longer than the official distance, it means that the course designer has measured the route more tightly than you have. As a result your minute markers will be slightly out and you will need to arrive at each

This is what I call a galloping fence. A sloping triple bar, which is straightforward and inviting, so you can gallop on into it. Obviously you do not want to ride recklessly at it, but you should not need to take a pull in front of it. Just let the horse jump it out of his stride.

This fence at the Seoul Olympics had a very steep downhill approach, and on both the landing and take-off sides the levels in the ground varied considerably. I eventually opted to jump the fence on the left where the ground for the take-off was slightly higher than the ground on the right.

When you jump a downhill fence like this it is important to make sure that you are straight going into it and that you keep your horse balanced all the way down the hill, not letting him fall onto his forehand. Do not over-check, however, otherwise you might end up pulling the horse to the base of the fence and making the jump more difficult for him. As long as you have your horse balanced well, these fences tend to jump better than you might think – provided, of course, that your horse is quite neat with his front legs.

marker a little earlier than planned. If you have measured the course shorter it means you have gone tighter than the official measurements and therefore your minute markers will be a little on the generous side.

By the time I do my third walk round I have more or less made up my mind where I am going to jump most of the fences. So this time I study the route that I am most likely to take, and also have another look at the alternatives. After that I have a very familiar picture of my line at each fence and the exact route I am taking to it. The third walk is usually completed on the Friday of the competition, and then if I feel I need to walk the course a fourth time I do it again either on Friday or first thing Saturday morning. The fourth walk is usually more of a confidence booster for the rider and also helps to fill in a bit of time. It is normally a fairly quick walk round, a final familiarisation of the planned route, and I always like to do this on my own so that I can concentrate one hundred per cent on what I am doing.

CHAPTER 9

Cross-country Riding Technique

By the time you come to ride a cross-country course, be it at a one-day or three-day event, you should know the route so well that you have a mental picture of how you are going to approach and jump each fence and how you will get to that fence. If you know the course well enough, you will automatically follow the correct line, and this leaves your mind free to concentrate on your approach to the next jump.

Remember that your mental attitude is very important. You need to be in a positive frame of mind before you set out on the course. How you achieve this is up to you. Some people like to sit on their own and concentrate, others prefer company – it depends on what suits your personality.

If there is a fence on the course that worries me I never think of not being able to jump that obstacle. Instead, I make myself think that I will have to ride that much better or that much stronger in order to negotiate it. If you entertain negative thoughts they will transmit themselves to the horse.

Your stirrup length for the cross-country should be set at a level that is comfortable, but should be short enough to enable you to keep your centre of balance over the horse's withers. Between fences it is best to stay out of the saddle and in balance with the horse, just letting him gallop on underneath you. Then, as you approach a fence, sit up and let your weight come down into the saddle five or six strides out from the fence. This helps to balance the horse, and your seat is then in a strong driving position should you need to use it.

I always carry a whip and ride in spurs. No matter how honest or genuine a horse is there may come a time when you have to use the stick or your spurs for a little persuasion, and it is bound to be the time when you are not carrying a stick that you need it most.

More often than not the stick is used as an encouragement rather than a punishment. If the horse is feeling a little tentative, then a slap with the stick may give him the extra confidence he needs to go on and do the job. If he is hanging back or he makes a bad jump over a fence, then I might give him a couple of reminders with the stick to get him going forward again and to re-focus his mind on the job. It is far better to do that than wait until the horse makes a serious mistake and you end up having a refusal or even a fall.

I have said all along that it is very important to keep a rhythm on the cross-country, but obviously there will be some fences on the course that

These two photos
show a correct
position over two
cross-country
obstacles. In the
first picture
(immediately
right) my lower leg
is in a slightly
better position, with
the weight well
down in the heel.
The contact is
maintained but is
not restricting the
horse. The angle of
the hip is closed,
and my body is low
to the horse and in
balance with him.
In both pictures the
horse is jumping
with a good shape.

The classic Lucinda
Green cross-country
seat. It looks as if
the horse has stood
well off the fence
and Lucinda has
adapted her seat to
cope. Her lower leg
is well forward, but
secure, and her seat
is in contact with
the horse. Her
upper body is
forward and she has
allowed the horse
complete freedom to
get on with the job.

Although this rider is negotiating the same fence safely, her general position gives an impression of insecurity. Her toes are down, and her knee and lower leg have come away from the horse and moved back. They are no longer in a strong position.

you have to approach at a slower pace. You will need to work out in advance the speed at which you are going to approach each obstacle, according to its type, its position and its complexity. While no two fences are exactly the same, there are some basic guidelines that you can follow in this respect, and the photographs in this chapter give examples of rider technique – good and bad – over a variety of fences.

Drop fences

Your pace will depend to some extent on the height of the drop, on whether the landing slopes away from you or rises up to meet you, and on whether it is off a downhill approach or a level approach. Basically,

Bold and safe riding over a fence with a big ditch and drop on the landing side. The rider has used her stick to encourage the horse to jump and is now in a good position to make a safe landing. Her weight is down in her heel; her lower leg is slightly forward and secure, and her upper body is in a good position for this stage of the jump.

Capt. Mark Phillips and Cartier coming off a drop fence. His lower leg is secure, although his weight could be down through his heel a little more. He has slipped the reins slightly and his upper body has come back a little to help balance the horse as it lands.

though, it is not a good idea to jump drop fences too fast. Steady the horse a little in front of the fence and make sure he is off his forehand, then keep coming forward in a steady rhythm.

If you go too fast over a drop fence you pitch more weight on to the horse's forehand and he is more likely to knuckle on landing or lose his balance. Coming in a little on the deep side of the take-off point helps the horse to see where he is going to land, and he is less likely to take fright and leave a leg behind as he takes off.

Never jump a drop fence at an angle. If a horse does by chance leave one front leg behind it can have the effect of spinning you sideways, giving you little hope of staying on board. If you take the fence straight, the horse will not twist so badly, and you might be able to stay together and avoid 60 penalties.

You will need to know how to slip your reins when you jump a drop fence. As your upper body comes back to prepare for the landing, you need to open your fingers slightly and allow the reins to slip through. It is a good idea to practise this, so that when you land, even though your reins are long, you can still maintain enough steering and control to ride away from the fence or to jump the next fence, if it follows on quickly. Although you may not need to slip your reins over every drop fence, if you never learn to slip them you will be caught out over big drop fences, where you are likely to be pulled right out of the saddle and over your horse's neck as he stretches his head forward and down to prepare for landing.

1   2

Jane Starkey showing how a water combination should be ridden.
1. Having slipped the reins, she is in a good, secure position to help the horse as he lands.
2. Her lower leg has not moved and she is in balance and looking towards the next fence.

This rider's stirrups are too long for my liking. The horse has made a bold jump into the water, and she
has done the correct thing by sitting back to balance the horse. However, both horse and rider land in a

3   4

3–4. Though her reins are still long, she is able to regulate the horse to guide him to the right spot to jump out of the water.

bit of a heap, and the rider is unable to organise herself and the horse before making a rather messy exit from the water.

American Anne Hardaway and Tarzan at the first water fence in Seoul. This combination make a good jump over the first element, but then Tarzan appears to back off the rail into the water. Anne sits down in the saddle so that she can use her seat and legs, and she also uses her stick in an effort to drive the horse over the fence. He then makes a good job of jumping into the water and Anne regains her normal position.

This sequence illustrates a good piece of aggressive cross-country riding. However, I would have liked to have seen Anne move her left hand back to the reins as she landed over the fence.

Lorna Clarke on Fearliath Mor gives an example of rescuing a tricky situation. The horse has jumped into the water well but appears to have taken off too far away from the bank going out. Lorna has put herself into a safety position, but is not interfering with the horse. His hind legs miss the bank, but because the horse is balanced and Lorna has a positive, forward-thinking attitude, the horse sorts himself

Water

The speed of approach to water obstacles depends very much on the depth of the water. If it is shallow, say about 6ins (15 cm) I almost disregard the water and simply ride the fence. However, if it is deep you have to be aware of the drag effect this can have on the horse. The deeper the water, the more difficult it is for the horse to move his front legs out of the way ready for the next stride – and if you have been going very fast you may be stopped in your tracks and end up taking a ducking. From your cross-country schooling, or from previous events, you will know how your horse reacts to water. If he is a little spooky you will need to ride him that much stronger. If he loves jumping water and makes big, bold leaps then you might have to ride him more cautiously.

As with drop fences, aim to bring your horse in fairly close to a fence going into water. If you try to jump it off a long stride, the horse may be tempted to put down again when he sees the water.

As you go through the water it is important to maintain whatever pace your horse gives you when he lands. It does not matter if he has come back to a trot, just keep him going in a forward, active trot; if the horse stays in canter, again leave him in that pace and keep him as balanced as you can through the water, waiting for the stride to come up to the next fence.

Uprights

On a galloping course these need care. You should not attempt to gallop at steeplechase speed into solid, upright fences because they can be quite

out and recovers well to jump the last element.

A cross-country rider can look good when everything is going right, but the really good riders and horses are the ones who are able to recover from seemingly hopeless situations.

difficult for a horse to judge. You should sit up, balance the horse and make sure of a correct stride into the fence.

Spreads   These can normally be jumped out of your galloping rhythm. However, some spreads are easier than others in this respect. Fences such as an oxer with a very upright front rail, or a hayrack, can sometimes have a false groundline, and these need to be ridden with care.

Jumping from light into dark   Jumping from light into dark can cause confusion because the horse may be busy peering into the darkness to see where he is going instead of concentrating on the fence. You need to bring the horse back, steady the rhythm, and give him time to see what he has to negotiate.

Banks and steps   Jumping up banks is similar to jumping uprights. Steady the horse, place his hocks well under him and try to come in fairly close to the base of the bank. If you stand a long way off a bank this tends to make the horse land rather flat on the top of the bank and, if it is a staircase-type obstacle, this can make it more difficult to negotiate the subsequent steps. As the horse goes up the bank you need to keep your weight forward and your seat off his back to allow him to bring his hind legs up and underneath him. Once you are up the first step it is important to keep driving forward so that the horse maintains his momentum up the remaining steps.

When you descend steps you need to have your centre of balance well back and your weight down in your heels; your lower leg should be slightly forward of the vertical, to keep the weight off your horse's

A nice sequence showing horse and rider in balance and harmony as they jump down a bank. The horse canters away happy and confident.

forehand and to help him balance on the way down. But you will also need to keep your leg on the horse so that if he hesitates you are in a position to drive him forward off the step.

Coffins

As a general rule these should be ridden in a strong, show-jumping type of canter, so that the horse's stride is shorter and rounder on the approach to the fence. A common mistake is failing to set up the horse early enough, with the result that the rider is still trying to organise the horse's stride as he approaches the fence. You must have the horse listening and under control in good time so that, in the last two or three strides, you can ride forward to the fence in a balanced rhythm. If you are still fighting to gain control when you come into the fence, the horse might interpret this as a request to stop, and he may very well oblige.

Combinations

Setting up a horse for a combination will depend very much on the layout of the obstacle. If it is a short-striding combination, then obviously you will have to bring your horse back into a short-striding rhythm. If there is a fairly long distance in the combination, you can afford to keep coming at a stronger pace.

Corners

These demand a lot of control. You cannot rely on speed to get you over. If your horse is at all wavery in holding a line you will need to have him at

A good position for descending steps. Ian Stark's lower leg and seat are secure. His upper body is back providing the balance, and his hands are allowing the horse freedom but at the same time maintaining a contact.

Rachel Hunt and Friday Fox make a rare mistake but escape unscathed. Friday has obviously lost her concentration and was perhaps too close to the first element; she has left a leg behind. Rachel sits very close to the horse and does not lose her position, and by the time they jump the second element of the combination they have almost regained their composure. Over the third element you would not know anything had gone wrong.

Wilton Fair and I at the same fence. The horse has started to drift to the right through this combination. You can see in the second photo that I have had to use my left rein to try to keep him straight for the approaching third element. When you are riding through combinations you must always be prepared to make adjustments to keep your horse on your chosen line.

A very tidy piece of riding from Tiny Clapham and Windjammer at Badminton. The position of Tiny's lower leg hardly alters at all, so she is able to stay in complete balance with the horse throughout this

Rider and horse narrowly escape disaster at the State Bank complex in Gawler. In the first picture the rider has allowed her body to get too far in front of the movement. Her seat has therefore come right out of the saddle, she has pivoted on her knee and her lower leg has swung back, making this a totally insecure position. The horse stretches across the ditch, but the rider has virtually no contact with the saddle.

difficult combination. The second photo shows the balancing position; the third one shows the driving position; and the fourth shows the take-off position.

The horse pecks slightly on landing and, because of the rider's insecure position, she is then shot forward up the horse's neck. She appears to be riding with her stirrups a little too long. However, being a survivor, this rider managed to sort herself out and the pair completed the combination without faults.

This photograph shows Wilton Fair near the end of the cross-country course at Burghley in 1987. We were travelling at speed and I had ridden for a long stride. A slap with the stick has helped to persuade him to take off and, because of the width of the oxer and the slight downhill landing, I have adopted an exaggerated safety position. However, I am still not interfering with the horse, and he has his ears pricked and is getting on with the job. You cannot look perfectly poised at every fence!

a pace in which you have plenty of control and he is truly between your hand and leg, like a strong show-jumping type of canter. Even so, make sure that you come in strongly and keep the forward momentum. Many people worry about corners so much that they over-check, then the horse loses his rhythm coming into the fence and he starts to think backwards. Once that happens it is easy for him to run out.

Uphill and downhill approaches

Negotiating uphill approaches is similar to jumping up steps in that you need to keep your weight forward to help the horse up the incline. More often than not a horse will meet a fence going up a hill on a correct stride.

When you approach a fence downhill, keep your upper body back to help balance the horse on the descent. A more collected canter will help the horse retain his balance.

CHAPTER 10 *Riding the Course*

Timing

Time is a crucial factor in the speed and endurance test. From the start of the roads and tracks on Phase A to the end of the cross-country, your timing has to be carefully worked out and your plan adhered to. If you go over the optimum time in any phase you will collect penalty points, but if you go too fast you will wear the horse out unnecessarily and jeopardise your chances of finishing the competition. Good time-keeping comes with experience, but if you have done your homework there is no reason why you should not get it right at your first three-day event.

At a one-day event, timing is less important and I never bother to time myself. I think it can be detrimental to ride one-day events to a stopwatch, particularly at advanced level, because it is almost impossible to achieve the optimum time anyway. If you are going for a fast time at an advanced one-day event then you will be going as fast as you safely can.

At a novice one-day event time should not be a major consideration. Initially you are going out to give the horse experience over different types of fence and to establish a rhythm. Later you can gradually increase that rhythm so that you arrive at the finish near to the optimum time. That way you will learn to judge the pace yourself and will not have to rely on a stopwatch to tell you how fast you are going. With practice, even when tackling a three-day event course, you should be able to ride without a stopwatch and finish close to the optimum time. It may, however, be a good idea for a novice rider aiming at his first three-day event to wear a stopwatch throughout a one-day event just to get used to the idea of looking at a watch and checking the time.

The timing on the steeplechase at a three-day event is usually very easy to work out as most courses are ridden in 4 minutes. If the required speed is 690m per minute simply measure every 690 metres of the course so that you have three check points before the finish. I normally use only a half-way point, as I have learned to be able to judge the speed fairly accurately.

Having established all the minute markers on the cross-country during my second course walk, I then pick out the convenient ones to use. Obviously if one of your markers comes 20 metres before a fence, this is not going to be a good time to look at your watch to check if you are on time or not. So the markers I use depend on where they are located and at what stage of the course. On a 10- or 11-minute cross-country ride, the first time check would probably come after 2 or 3 minutes, the second after 5 or 6 minutes and the third at around 8 or even 9 minutes. After that it is very difficult to make up much time if you are behind schedule.

*Working out
speed and
endurance times*

In the schedule you will be given the distance, speed and optimum times of all four phases. For example:

PHASE	NATURE	DISTANCE km	m	SPEED m/min	OPTIMUM TIME hr	mins	secs
A	Roads and Tracks	5	940	220		27	00
B	Steeplechase	3	105	690		4	30
C	Roads and Tracks	6	380	220		29	00
	Veterinary Inspection					10	00
D	Cross-Country	6	840	570		12	00
	TOTAL	22	265		1	22	30

You will also be supplied with a list of competitors' start times which are made to correspond with the schedule. They will read something like this:

COMPETITOR	START PHASE A	FIN A/START B	FIN B/START C	FIN C	START D	FIN D
1. Mark Todd (Bahlua)	9.00	9.27	9.31.30	10.00.30	10.10.30	10.22.30
2. Martha Mad (Rising Moon)	9.04	9.31	9.35.30	10.04.30	10.14.30	10.26.30

I normally write my times on a card, slip it into a plastic case and strap it on to my arm with velcro; some riders tape the card on to their arm; others simply write the information straight on their skin. If it is wet, though, the latter method is not reliable because the ink tends to run. Do not make this job too complicated: write down only the information that you need. And remember to leave space at the sides of the chart for the tape, if that is how you are planning to attach it to your arm.

The opposite page shows how I would write out my times to coincide with the schedule above.

I do not write down anything for Phase D because if I had time to read my card I wouldn't be concentrating on my ride. This *has* to be committed to memory.

**Roads and
tracks
(Phase A)**

The speed required on the roads and tracks is 220m per minute, which is roughly equivalent to a good brisk trot. This speed works out at approximately 1 kilometre in 4 minutes, so if you cover the ground at that rate you should finish Phase A with around 2 minutes to spare. If you have never done a three-day event before, it would probably pay you to measure out a couple of kilometres and see how long it takes you to ride them at different paces, so that you can get a feel of the sort of speed at which you will need to go. The time is fairly lenient.

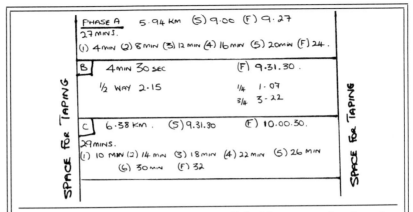

PHASE A   5·94 KM   (S) 9·00 (F) 9·27
27 MINS.
(1) 4 MIN (2) 8 MIN (3) 12 MIN (4) 16 MIN (5) 20 MIN (F) 24.

B   4 MIN 30 SEC   (F) 9·31·30 .
     ½ WAY 2·15   ¼   1·07
                               ¾   3·22

C   6·38 KM .   (S) 9·31·30   (F) 10·00·30.
29 MINS.
(1) 10 MIN (2) 14 MIN (3) 18 MIN (4) 22 MIN (5) 26 MIN
        (6) 30 MIN   (F) 32

SPACE FOR TAPING

SPACE FOR TAPING

For **Phase A** I do not normally write out all the kilometre marker times, but you can if you think you will need them. These times will get me in three minutes before I am due to start the 'chase.

For **Phase B** you may want to put the quarter way and threequarter way times; or you may have measured the course for every minute marker.

Again, on **Phase C** you can write out all the kilometre marker times if you feel you need them. I find that working them out as I go gives me something to do to relieve the boredom of the roads and tracks. Here I have allowed 5 mins 30 secs for the first kilometre and have added on the 4 mins 30 secs of the steeplechase, giving a total of 10 mins. After that I have gone back to my 4 mins per kilometre, finishing with my stopwatch showing 32 mins. The actual time taken for Phase C (less the 4 mins 30 secs) is 27 mins 30 secs, or 1½ mins under the optimum time of 29 mins. If, for any reason, you are delayed at the start of A, you may want to set your normal watch back so that it reads the time that you should have started, so that your start and finish times will not be altered.

I like to begin the first section of roads and tracks (Phase A) by asking the horse to trot along at a good pace. Then, at some point where the going is good (I will have earmarked this when driving round the course), I let the horse have a canter for 400–500 metres to warm him up for the steeplechase. This has the effect of putting you ahead of time, so you can then afford a short walk before you reach the end of Phase A. I like to reach the finish two or three minutes before I am due to start the steeplechase, so that there is enough time to check the girths and make sure everything is all right. If you arrive too early you have to do a lot of waiting around before starting the steeplechase. If you arrive late, you will incur penalty points.

Steeplechase (Phase B)

Once you have gone into the start box for Phase B, the steeplechase, make sure that the horse is awake and ready to jump out as soon as the starter tells you to go. Some horses become excited once they know what it is all about, so it may be best not to keep them standing in the box for too long. As you start out of the box remember to set your stopwatch and then get the horse galloping at steeplechase speed straight away. Do not let your

Riders synchronising their watches with the master clock at the start of phase A.

Checking my watch on the roads and tracks.

Left: *At the start of the steeplechase with Welton Greylag*. Right: *Getting away to a flying start*.

horse gradually wind up to the desired speed, otherwise you will find that at the end of the course you have to go very fast to catch up on the time wasted. It depends on your horse's attitude, but you may have to kick him on or give him one with the stick to get his mind on the job and get him galloping properly.

It takes experience to know how fast you should go, so it is a good idea to practise galloping with someone else to accustom yourself to the right speed. If you set your horse at this speed as soon as you leave the start box, then all you have to do is sit as still as you possibly can and jump the fences within the rhythm you have established.

Initially it takes a fair amount of nerve to sit there and do nothing as you approach a fence at a fast gallop, but you will learn to see a stride out of that gallop and the horse will adjust himself to jumping at that speed. Avoid the temptation to slow down and set your horse up for each fence, as this will interrupt the rhythm. Train him instead to gallop into his steeplechase fences and jump them out of his stride. This is the easiest way to get round the steeplechase course within the optimum time.

The same principle applies to cross-country riding: keep your horse in a rhythm and adjust your stride out of that rhythm. The only difference on the steeplechase is that you are doing it a bit faster. If you leave a horse entirely alone and come into a fence in a galloping rhythm, eight times out of ten the striding will come right. The other two times you may have to kick on a little to lengthen your horse's stride slightly, or you may have to sit and hold for a second to get in the extra stride. Always wait for the fence to come to you, and then adjust the stride if you have to.

Ginny Leng and Priceless on the steeplechase in Los Angeles. Ginny has a good forward seat, with her head up.

If you watch top steeplechase jockeys you will see that the best ones interfere very little with their horses during a race. Generally speaking, the more still you can sit, the better the horse will go.

You should stay out of the saddle the whole way, balancing over your horse's shoulder. On the steeplechase I normally ride a hole or two shorter than I do on the cross-country because the rider's point of balance is a bit further forward when a horse is going faster.

As you finish the steeplechase let your horse come back to a trot gradually. Do not pull him up abruptly as soon as you go through the finish, and do not throw the reins away and let him fall back into trot. Keeping him together, bring him back to a steady canter and then back to trot. If your horse is a little tired and you allow him to fall into trot or pull him up sharply, you risk causing damage to the tendons.

At this stage I do not usually worry about re-setting my stopwatch.

Jeremy Spring on Holy Smoke show a good position for landing: heels down, weight back and arms stretched forward to allow the body to come back without interfering with the horse.

Once it has been set at the start of Phase B I let it continue running right through to the end of Phase C. This means that the time allowed for the steeplechase has to be added on to your Phase C times. For example, if the steeplechase was 4 minutes and you are allowing 5 minutes for your first kilometre on Phase C, your stopwatch will read 9 minutes at the 1-kilometre marker. I prefer to do this because it is very easy to forget to reset your watch at the end of the steeplechase, and then you can end up getting into a muddle with your times. (See diagram on page 125 for calculating times and setting stopwatch.)

You should pull up from the steeplechase just in time for the assistance point, which is normally about 400 metres beyond the finish of the steeplechase. This is the only place on the speed and endurance, apart from the ten-minute box, where you are allowed outside assistance.

If the weather is very hot, I like to have a groom waiting at the assistance point with a bucket of water. We can then sponge the horse's neck and maybe sponge out his mouth, but I certainly would not let the horse have a drink as this could upset his stomach. In cases of extreme heat, such as we experienced at the Seoul Olympics and the Stockholm World Championships, I make sure that my groom at the assistance point has a small cloth bag full of ice which I can carry with me on Phase C. I can then hold the bag of ice on the horse's poll area and also rub it up and down his neck to help cool him.

Equipment for end of steeplechase

Bucket and sponge (check that water is available at the assistance point)
Spare set of shoes (with studs in place *)
Equiboot
Spare bridle
Spare girths
Spare leathers and irons
Something to drink (for rider)

* Most three-day events have roads and tracks with good surfaces, but if the ground is very hard, or a lot of road work is involved, I would probably leave the studs off my horse's shoes until the ten-minute halt.

This short break provides an opportunity to look the horse over quickly and to check all the shoes before moving off again. At most three-day events there is a blacksmith on hand, so it is a good idea for your assistant to have a spare set of shoes with him at the end of the steeplechase. If you have pulled a shoe and there is no blacksmith, you can put on an Equiboot or some other kind of hoof protection that will allow you to finish the roads and tracks without damaging the horse's foot. You can usually have the shoe put back on during the ten-minute halt.

Roads and tracks (Phase C)

Phase C is always longer than Phase A, but the speed required is the same, so you can work roughly to your 4 minutes per kilometre timing. However, I normally allow 10 or 11 minutes to cover the first 2 kilometres because of the extra time taken at the assistance point and also because I like the horse to walk for a fair bit of the first kilometre to recover his respiration rate. After that I increase the pace again and return to my average speed of 4 minutes per kilometre to the end of the phase.

Some people like to hop off their horses and run beside them on roads and tracks, which can be a good idea, but you must remember that you have to be mounted as you pass through the start and finish flags of Phase A and C.

Exceeding the optimum time on the roads and tracks is unnecessary and usually the result of bad planning. It is also very expensive because you incur a penalty point for every second that you exceed the stipulated time.

This is more severe than on either the cross-country (where you incur 0.4 penalties for each second over) or the steeplecase (0.8 penalties for each second over). If you exceed the time limit (usually twice the optimum time) on any of the phases you will be eliminated.

The ten-minute halt

As you approach the ten-minute halt box at the end of Phase C you will be asked to trot on a loose rein for the last 100 metres of roads and tracks, to allow a veterinary panel to see if your horse is sound. The panel, which consists of a veterinary surgeon and two officials, has the right to eliminate any horse considered unfit to continue. Once you have passed the finish you will be asked to dismount, and a vet will quickly check the pulse and respiration rates of the horse. All being well, you are then free to take the horse away (within the confines of the box) to look after him.

It is a good idea to be familiar with your own horse's normal pulse rate and rate of recovery because these can vary a great deal from one horse to another. In a competition atmosphere a horse's pulse is likely to be higher than normal because he is more excited. A horse's recovery rate is an indication of how fit he is, but it is also affected by his temperament. Southern Comfort had a remarkable recovery rate. At Badminton in 1980 his pulse had dropped back to normal only five minutes after he came off Phase C, which is exceptional. He was very fit, but he was also a relaxed

A vet checking the heart rate after the horse has come off phase C.

sort of horse. Funnily enough, he had a heart murmur, and when he was completely at rest his heart sometimes skipped a beat. Fortunately once he started working he was fine.

Equipment for ten-minute halt box

You should have all the equipment that was taken to the end of steeplechase *plus*:
Another bucket
Sweat scraper
Towels
Halter and lead rope
String cooler
Wool blanket
Rainsheet (if the weather looks doubtful)
Spare overreach boots
Spare leg boots
Grease and glove with which to apply it
Basic veterinary kit, including wound powder, support bandages and underwraps (if the injury is serious there will be a vet on hand to treat the horse).
If it is very hot you should arrange to have ice available in the box.
Some people like a chair to sit on.

You need a couple of helpers on hand in the box, one to hold your horse and another to attend to him. There are often restrictions on the number of people allowed in the area, and anyway, if you have too many assistants trying to help they will probably get in each other's way. Some events limit you to only one groom, but there are nearly always other people around who can help out and offer advice.

If it is raining, quickly put a waterproof rug over the horse to protect him from the cold and wet. I do not feel it is necessary to remove the saddle – it then takes you that much longer to get it back on again – just loosen off the girth and noseband. Quickly sponge the horse down, washing between the hind legs, and sponge out the mouth. Do not put any water over the horse's back or loins, as this can cause cramping of the muscles on a hot horse. Basically, you are just freshening up the horse.

If the horse is wearing bandages, with gamgee underneath them, it is a good idea to tie a towel above the knee to stop the water running down into the bandages. After you have washed down the horse make sure that you dry the reins well so that you do not start the cross-country with wet, slippery reins. Scrape the horse off and quickly rub him dry, then throw a cooling sheet over him if it is hot, or, if it is cold, woollen rugs to keep him warm. The whole procedure wants to be completed very quickly, within a matter of one or two minutes; after that keep the horse moving.

When it is very hot or humid try to cool the horse down as much as

Washing the horse down during the ten-minute halt.

possible by holding ice-packs on him at points where there is the most blood flow – around the poll region, on the jugular vein and between the back legs. At the Olympic Games in Los Angeles (in 1984) a lot of riders used fans to help cool down their horses at the end of Phase C and at the end of the cross-country.

After about five minutes the vet will come back to check the horse's respiration rate. Then, with about four minutes left to go, the horse has grease daubed on his legs (I do not apply grease for the steeplechase). Greasing the legs has dubious benefits, but it is something I have always done. The idea is that if a horse does hit a fence or catch a leg, he will slip over the fence more easily and suffer less damage, and he is also less likely to fall. Once the greasing is complete the noseband is done up, the saddle moved forward and the girth tightened. With two minutes to go I hop on the horse and give him a trot and a canter around the area just to loosen him up again so that he is ready to start the cross-country.

There will usually be a steward in the ten-minute box to tell you that you have, say, five minutes to go and to count down the minutes until your departure, but if there isn't one, make sure that one of your helpers

Applying grease to the horse's legs before the cross-country.

checks with the time-keeper and watches the clock for you. Although ten minutes may seem a long time it actually goes very quickly and you do not want to be rushing at the last minute to get to the start. The starter will normally tell you that you have one minute to go and call you into the starting area.

How soon you go into the start box will depend on your horse's temperament. I normally like to walk the horse round in front of the starting box until I have about twenty seconds to go, and then I walk into the box and stand quietly. If the horse is a little up-tight, stroke his neck and talk to him. With a very fractious horse it can be a good idea to ask someone to lead him into the start box and to stand there with him. You will be counted down from either ten or five seconds. Then press your stopwatch and away you go.

On Phase A, B and C I wear a stopwatch and an ordinary watch, but I do not usually bother with a spare stopwatch. I have done so many three-day events now that I know more or less how fast I am going. There is always a clock at the beginning of Phase A, and you can check your watch with the starter to make sure that it is synchronised. If your stopwatch then fails you at least know at what time you are supposed to be where. For the cross-country I normally remove my ordinary watch and rely entirely on my stopwatch. Make sure that you have reset your stopwatch after Phase C.

The cross-country (Phase D)

The way you set about riding the cross-country course will depend on the conditions – the weather, the state of the ground, the length of the course – and on whether you are going out to win the competition or are content just to get round (it may be your first three-day event, or you may be riding a relatively novice horse). If you are riding for a team at an international event your approach will be influenced by the needs of your team and the instructions from your chef d'équipe. Whatever the circumstances, it is essential that you set out on the cross-country as if you mean business.

I like the horse to leave the start box and set off in a good rhythm straight away. Even if I am not intending to go particularly fast, I never let the horse amble out of the start box. The horse needs to understand that he has a job ahead, so have him going away from your leg so that he is taking you by the hands. This is particularly important with green horses who do not really know what is going on. They can be a bit hesitant and wander aimlessly out of the start box. If they do not pick up straight away, give them a reminder with the stick to help focus their minds and get them going forward. You should immediately establish the rhythm you want to maintain for the rest of the course. Most people lose time in the first few minutes because they do not get the horse going at a good pace as soon as they come out of the box.

If you are aiming to go round within the optimum time, you need to be at your first minute marker on time, and you must try to keep to your time markers all the way round the course. Once you get behind, it is difficult to make up time. However, you may have to make allowances for certain factors that will affect your speed. For example, a part of the course that has a lot of combinations or a lot of fences in quick succession will ride more slowly than parts where there is open galloping. You should have considered all this when you walked the course, noting the places where you are likely to be slowed down and where you will be able to make up time. Even so, the easiest way to achieve the optimum time is to stick to your time markers as closely as possible and to keep your horse going in a regular rhythm.

Stopping and starting is very tiring for a horse, so the more flowing your round, the more energy you are going to conserve. This is important even at novice one-day event level. If you slow down to jump each fence and gallop fast in between, it is very taxing on the horse. You will also find that a horse who goes flat out between his fences but then has to be pulled up 200 metres in front of an obstacle in order to jump it safely will probably be slower overall than one who keeps a steady rhythm all the way round. One classic example of the latter was a horse called Wilton Fair, on whom I won Burghley in 1987. Although he was not a fast galloper, he was so well balanced and neat that I never had to check him, and thus I could still achieve a good time with him.

There is no point in starting a cross-country course faster than necessary as you run the risk of your horse being tired towards the end, and once the horse is tired he is more likely to make mistakes in his jumping, and more likely to cause injury to himself. This is why you should set out at the speed that you want to maintain for the most part of the course. Keep an eye on your time checks and try to stick to them, but if your horse starts to feel as if he is getting tired then you will have to ease up a little. It is no good pushing on regardless as you run the risk of damaging your horse, or, even worse, having a fall and hurting both yourself and the horse.

Riding a tired horse can be a new experience for a lot of people. This is where you need to be thinking all the time: there may be a difficult combination near the end of the course where you had planned to take the direct route, but if your horse is tired it may be sensible to change your plan and go the longer, safer way. This is why it is important when walking the course to study *every* option at *every* fence, so that if you do have to make a change of plan, you know exactly what you are going to do. A tired horse needs a lot more leg and also needs balancing in the hand to keep him together.

You must ride according to the conditions. If it is very hot and humid the organisers will sometimes have made allowances for this by shortening the roads and tracks or the steeplechase, but as an individual you must assess how well your horse can cope with the distance under the conditions on the day. If the ground is very muddy, for example, it will be much more tiring for your horse than firm going. If at any stage you feel your horse is not right, the worst thing you can do is carry on regardless, as you are likely to be riding for a fall as well as risking your horse's career.

Falls

If you do have a fall it is best to try to stay relaxed. Steeplechase jockeys will tell you to curl into a ball so that you roll on landing rather than hit the ground with a thump. Most injuries, particularly broken collar-bones, are caused by the rider automatically putting his hand out to save himself. It is an instinctive thing to do. You do not usually get time to think, but you should try to crumple on landing.

If you are not seriously hurt and your horse has not run off, get up and check him over for cuts, and then trot him up to see if he is sound. When you get back on, trot for a few strides just to check again that he is sound, and then canter away. All being well, I like to try to carry on as I think it is better for the horse. It helps to regain his confidence straight away (and yours), but if the horse does not go well, you should pull up.

You can usually relate a fall to something you have done. More often than not it is the rider's fault, but you do sometimes come across a horse who just does not seem to like standing on his own four feet. A good event horse needs some sense of self-preservation, and if a horse keeps falling he is not worth riding. No matter how good a rider you are, if you start having a lot of bad falls it does not do your confidence any good.

I used to ride a horse called Jocasta, who gave me a lot of falls, and I reckon it took me about five years to get over that horse. If you have too many falls you start riding for them; you keep doublechecking that you are doing everything right, becoming over-cautious. Then, because of that, you start losing your rhythm and you are more inclined to make mistakes.

A fall at Belton Park with Jued Lad. It happened at the fourth fence, a straightforward haywagon. The horse was not looking where he was going, and galloped straight in to it, chesting it. You can usually find a reason for a fall, and more often than not it is the rider's fault. In this case, I had not warmed up Jued Lad properly before the start of the cross-country and he did not have his mind on the job.

Having a lot of falls when you are young is not too bad because you have more nerve, but when you get a bit older you start to realise that you want to preserve yourself! You have to be able to trust your horse to a certain extent, and as soon as you start to get frightened about what might happen, it is time to give up.

There is usually a lesson to be learned from a fall. I had a bad tumble at Belton Park one-day event with Jued Lad, which seemed, on the face of it, to be totally his fault, but I later realised that it was really mine. As we came into the fourth fence, a straightforward, haywagon-type obstacle, he was not looking where he was going and galloped straight into it, chesting it. I could feel it was going to happen a couple of strides in front of the fence, but there was nothing I could do.

This horse and rider are in trouble over this upright fence with a downhill approach and landing. The picture shows what classically happens when a horse leaves one front leg on the jump (in this case the near fore). The horse's momentum spins the horse's body sideways, off balance, and hitting the dirt is almost inevitable.

It was my fault because I had not warmed up the horse properly and had not made sure he had his mind on the job. He had done his dressage and show jumping the day before, and he was one of the first to go across country the following morning. I had not taken into account the fact that he had done no dressage or show jumping to loosen him up before the cross-country, and I just popped him over a few fences before we set off. Also, because we were competing *hors concours*, I do not think I approached the course with the right mental attitude.

I learned two valuable lessons: firstly, always warm up your horse well before the cross-country in a one-day event: and, secondly, never go out for a casual school, especially if you are riding an advanced course. You must be switched on. Always treat a cross-country course with respect and attack it in a competitive and positive frame of mind.

The fall I had at Badminton in 1981 with Jocasta at the Elephant Trap was also my fault because the horse should never have been there in the first place. He had lost his confidence the year before and had not gone at all well in the spring events leading up to Badminton, but because I had won Badminton the previous year and because my parents were coming over to watch me, I felt that I had to have a runner. Southern Comfort had had to be withdrawn, so I took Jocasta in the hope that he would be all right on the day. But you cannot go to Badminton on that basis, and I learned another lesson the hard way. Jocasta was not confident enough. He put in an extra stride in front of the fence, caught his knees and down he went.

Sometimes falls are caused by a simple error of judgment on the part of the rider. This is always a difficult thing to admit, but mistakes do happen.

One of the hardest fences for a horse to judge is a bank out of water – usually because the horse kicks up so much spray in front of him as he travels towards it. This horse has obviously misjudged the bank, and has tripped and fallen on it.

My fall at Burghley with Nightlife in 1984 was down to me, though if the horse had been more clever I might have got away with it. The fence in question consisted of a very small step up on to a bank, then a bounce over a gap between the first bank and a second, bigger bank. I missed my stride coming in, panicked and rode for a long one. Because the first bank was so small there was nothing to make the horse jump up on to it properly, and he sort of paddled on to it, so he was not balanced enough to jump on to the next bank. He took a stride, stood on an over-reach boot, and as his front feet left the first bank he had nothing with which to push himself up; he went straight into the second bank. We made a complete mess of it. If the horse had taken off when I asked him and jumped cleanly on to the first bank, we would have been all right, but I could not blame him for getting it wrong. I had made the classic mistake of losing my head and trying to ride for a long stride.

My fall in the water at the World Championships in Gawler in 1986 was a result partly of poor information and partly my own bad judgment. I knew that Tinks Pottinger had successfully jumped the water complex over the route that I had planned to take, but I did not realise that nearly everyone else had jumped the fence more easily on the extreme right, where the distance between the drop and the rail in the water was long enough to fit in a short stride. This would probably have suited Charisma better, but because Tinks had managed the bounce I assumed we could do it too. I should have known better, because Charisma is a very different sort of horse to Tinks' big-striding Volunteer.

I did not see a good stride coming into the first rail. I met it on a slow, short stride, and then had to chase for the one stride to the drop into the water. Charisma put in an extra half stride and did not jump cleanly off the bank, which meant that he landed short, thus the distance was too long for him to bounce out over the rail. He reached for it and bellied it, and we both took a ducking.

You need a certain amount of luck on a cross-country course. Sometimes you get away with a near miss; sometimes you have a fall when you do not really deserve one. It's just the way it goes.

Retirements and eliminations

If you have had to retire or have been eliminated on the cross-country you should take your horse straight off the course and back to the stable. It is always a tremendous blow to have to retire a horse from an event, but you should never let the prospect of such a disappointment cloud your judgment. If your horse is not going well and not enjoying himself, you must use your discretion about pulling him up. To see a horse stopping all the time and having to be beaten over the fences is no fun for the spectators and does not do the image of the sport any good. It does not do you or your horse any good either, and it would probably be better to call it a day and have another go some other time. It is, incidentally, against the rules to continue after a third fall on the cross-country.

Finishing the course

Assuming that all has gone well and you have completed the course without problems, remember that no matter how delighted you are at having got round, you should never drop your reins and throw your arms around your horse's neck before you have pulled up. Keep the horse balanced and pull him up gradually to reduce the risk of injury. It is easy to break down a horse through something simple like pulling up badly at the end of a course.

Once you have ridden through the finish of a three-day event you will be escorted to the weighing-in area. You are not allowed outside assistance until you have weighed in correctly. You can use your saddle, your weight cloth, your bridle and even your martingale if necessary to make up the weight, but if you are still underweight you will be eliminated.

At a three-day event a vet will sometimes attend your horse again before it is cleared to go back to the stables, otherwise you will just be told that it is all right for you to go. As soon as you have weighed in, have a good look over the horse to see if he has any cuts or nicks, or any grazed skin. Put on a sweat rug or, if it is cold, a blanket, and keep the horse walking until he stops blowing. Normally there is a reasonably long walk back to the stables

Weighing-in at the end of the cross-country and signing the official's record.

and the horse should have more or less recovered his breathing by the time you get back. If the weather is very cold I like to wash a horse off with warm water. On a warm day he can be washed off with cold water.

In hot and humid conditions it is very important to get your horse cooled down as quickly as possible. Make use of any areas of shade that you can; apply water liberally; hold ice-packs against the horse where the blood vessels are closest to the surface – the poll, the jugular vein and inside the back legs.

When the horse has cooled down a little and stopped blowing, offer him some water, but not too much to start with. He can have another drink after about 15 minutes. You should avoid letting your horse gulp down a huge bucket of water straight away, as this can cause a colicky condition. If your horse shows any signs of distress, call for veterinary assistance.

Once the horse is back in his stable and has completely cooled down (usually after about an hour) he can have as much as he wants to drink. At this stage, provided my horse is all right, I like him to be led out for a bite of grass, so that he can unwind and relax for half an hour.

Any cuts or injuries should be treated as soon as you return to the stables. Simple cuts can be cleaned and dusted with wound powder, but anything more serious should be attended to by a veterinary surgeon. Check for over-reaches and for any swelling – if a horse is going to have tendon trouble it will have already started to show. Any filling in the legs at this stage should be treated immediately with cold water or ice. You can run a hose of cold water over the horse's leg or apply ice using a stretchy, stockinette bandage. Wurly boots can also be used (see page 60). Ask the vet to have a look at the problem as soon as possible so that you can get his opinion on it.

By now an hour has probably elapsed since the horse finished the cross-country, and this is a good time to give him a jog up to make sure that he is sound. The horse is unlikely to trot up as freely as he normally does but, provided he is taking level steps, he should be all right. Then the horse can go back to the stable for a bran mash with a small feed and a haynet.

I like to put kaolin poultices on the horse's legs, leaving them on overnight. If there is time, the horse will probably go out for another walk and a pick of grass before his evening feed. I will trot him up again, probably at about eight or nine o'clock, for a final check. By now you can expect the horse to have stiffened up quite a bit, but there is no point in trying to walk off the stiffness at this stage. I am a great believer in letting a horse have a good night's rest, and I do not advocate, under any circumstances, keeping the horse up walking all night. It is much better to leave him in peace, let him have a quiet night and then start work on him early in the morning.

The final horse inspection

You can more or less assume that if your horse is in a reasonable condition on the evening after the speed and endurance he will be all right the following morning. If you had any worries the night before, you would have called the vet, and, if you did, the vet will probably come again in the morning to check the horse and advise you on the best course of action.

Trotting up Bahlua at the final horse inspection at Badminton, 1990.

I like to take the horse out of the stable about three hours before the final horse inspection. He is walked out of the box and trotted up straight away, as this gives me a fair idea of how stiff he is and what will need to be done to loosen him up in readiness for the vet check. After that he can go back to his stable to have his breakfast, and then come out again to have the kaolin washed off his legs. If the horse was fine at his first trot-up, dry bandages are put back on; but if he was a touch lame, he is taken for an in-hand walk to see if the lameness will wear off. If it does not, you are in trouble, as there is not much you can do about it.

Any unevenness caused by stiffness can usually be walked or ridden out of the horse. It can be a good idea to go out for a ride round the area, or even round part of the cross-country. Just taking the horse out into the competition atmosphere again will make him perk up, and he will loosen up straight away with a bit of trotting and cantering. Once you have the horse out, keep him moving, even if just in walk, to make sure that he does not stiffen up again before he is presented to the Ground Jury. Make sure, though, that the horse does not arrive at the inspection in a sweating mess, because the Ground Jury will immediately suspect that there is something wrong with the horse and that you have been working hard on him to disguise it.

The way you present your horse at these inspections is very important. A horse needs to be taught how to trot up properly in-hand, and this should be done at home, not at the competition. Nothing looks worse than a rider having to drag his horse along at an inspection or, alternatively, having a horse leaping about on the end of the bridle and not trotting in a straight line. If the horse is lazy then practise at home by asking somebody to chase him up with a stick so that the horse learns to trot up correctly beside you. Try to keep the horse straight, and avoid using a stick yourself at the event, as this sometimes makes the horse shy away from you. If the horse does not trot straight, it can give the impression of being unlevel.

Most Juries like you to trot the horse on a loose rein, so do not be tempted to hold the horse's head up as you will only be asked to go again. At most inspections you will be told to walk the horse away from the Jury, then trot to the end of the designated area, and then turn round and trot back. Make the whole thing look business-like. Look ahead, do not look anxiously at your horse otherwise this will attract the Ground Jury's attention to him. When you reach the end, come back to a walk, turn the horse away from you and keep him at a steady walk. Then make sure he is straight again before you ask him to trot back towards the Jury. If you whizz your horse round too quickly he is likely to look unlevel.

CHAPTER 11

A Badminton Round

The 1990 Badminton Horse Trials was one of the hottest on record with the temperature on speed and endurance day in the 70°s. Fortunately there was a breeze blowing, so the horses did not find the conditions too bad, and a good number completed the cross-country within the optimum time because the ground was firm and the course was shorter than usual. (This was because the World Championships were taking place only eleven weeks after Badminton.) The event was won by Nicola McIrvine on Middle Road. I finished well down the field, in nineteenth place, with Bahlua, and retired Michaelmas Day after a fall on the cross-country. It was not my best Badminton.

Roads and tracks

Most of the roads and tracks at Badminton go through woods, so there is plenty of shade from the sun. Although this is not normally an important consideration at Badminton, it was significant in 1990 because of the exceptional heat. When I went down Worcester Avenue (an impressive avenue in the centre of Badminton Park) on Michaelmas Day, my first horse, I rode on the usual path on the left-hand side because at that time of day there was plenty of shade. However, by the afternoon, when I set out on Bahlua, the sun had moved to the other side, so I rode down the right-hand side to be in the shade. Worcester Avenue is about 3km long, so it did help to be able to trot along in the shade rather than in the full glare of the sun.

Steeplechase

The steeplechase was shorter than usual, so instead of a figure-of-eight, riders simply had to complete two circuits of the track – which at least was easy to remember. I had great rides with both my horses. They just bowled along on the firm going, and it was quite easy to make the time.

The cross-country

The first fence, the **Whitbread Barrels**, was sited only a short distance from the start, down a slight hill, so although it was a straightforward obstacle I did not want to crack on too fast. I just leapt out of the start box, cleared the fence and moved up a gear on the long gallop in front of Badminton House, setting the pace that I wanted to maintain around the course.

Fence 1
Whitbread Barrels

Wherever possible, it is always best to take the straightest line between fences, but obviously if there are any bad patches of ground you have to adjust your route slightly. This is the sort of thing that I check out when walking the course. For my approach to the second fence, the **Stick Pile**, I decided that the best line was to go inside the tree on the track and jump the fence slightly to the left.

Fence 2
Stick Pile

The turn into the **Deer Park Leap**, fence 3, was quite tight so it was necessary to balance the horse on the corner without actually slowing him down. I wanted to keep him coming off the corner and into the fence. As long as the horse is balanced you can wait for your stride into a fence like

Fence 3
Deer Park Leap

this and then ride for it. Although there was a big ditch on the landing side with a slight drop, I knew that the horses would not see it until they were in the air, so I rode it like a simple upright and it was fine.

The fourth fence was the **Tokyo Crossing**. This is a fence without a ground-line, but it is a very solid-looking obstacle and one that usually jumps well, even though the flowerboxes are off-set. When I walked the course I decided to aim for the second flowerbox from the right and to jump it in the centre. This was the most direct line, and also, being a slightly staggered fence, I thought it best to aim at something square on the near side. If you ride straight at one of the flowerboxes in the front row the horse jumps the fence quite happily and does not worry about the gap behind.

Fence 4
Tokyo Crossing

The most direct route at the **Beefeater Bridge**, fence 5, was over a big oxer set at an angle to a ditch. The ditch made a V-shape with the footbridge both on take-off and on landing, which meant that the horse had to jump more or less from the point of one V to another. This required considerable accuracy, but there was a little room for deviation to left or right. There were two alternatives: a straightforward oxer just to the right of the direct route, followed by a sharp left turn to the ditch; or an even longer way round over a bounce and then a stride to the ditch.

Fence 5
Beefeater Bridge

I decided to go for the quick option (over the corner) on both my horses. To do this, I had to follow the right-hand line of the string beside the course and then swing well to the right before coming into the fence.

When I walked the course here I had to keep reminding myself that I would need to swing out further right than seemed necessary when I first approached the fence. In the background, beyond the bridge, were three big trees, and the centre one lined up very well for the line I wanted. It was necessary to jump the bridge at a slight angle otherwise we should have landed in the ditch.

An experienced horse who does not mind ditches would not find the Beefeater Bridge too difficult. In fact most horses jump it without any problems as long as they can keep a straight line. The critical moment is coming off the turn. You have to sit up, balance your horse and look for your stride, but keep the horse moving; do not take a check and break his rhythm. You must keep coming to a fence like this because it is big, and the angled ditch makes it very wide.

My three-minute marker, which was my first time check, came about 200 yards in front of the next fence, the **Splash Pond Oxer**. When I looked at my stop-watch here on both horses I was doing fine – just under three minutes.

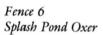

Fence 6
Splash Pond Oxer

From the take-off side, the Splash Pond Oxer was a fairly innocuous-looking fence, but there was a ditch on the landing side, so it had to be ridden positively in order to help the horse jump out over the ditch. I took it on the right where the ditch was smaller and there was less of a drop. It had to be jumped slightly from right to left because it was set at an angle to the course and there was a rail running alongside it on the right. But there was a tendency for the horses to drift a bit to the left anyway, because the ground sloped that way. As long as the fence was approached on the right-hand side it rode quite well, but it was still a big, wide obstacle that had to be treated with respect.

The first thing that struck me as I approached the **White Label Water Garden**, fences 7 and 8, on my initial course walk was that as the horses came down towards the two brush fences into the water, the grandstand on the far side of the fence would be right in their sight line. On Saturday it would be full of people and this might distract my horse's attention. So, on the approach, I would want to make sure that he was listening to me and not watching what was going on in the distance.

It was a big fence, but it looked as if the horses would not see the water until, I hoped, it was too late. I knew that I would want to ride it fairly

Francesca Golding and Western Point negotiating the White Label Water Garden (fence 8). This was where I had my fall with Michaelmas Day. You had to bounce over a brush fence into the water. Michaelmas Day jumped over the second brush quite well, but his back end disappeared from under him as he touched down in the water; he pitched right and I was shot out of the saddle.

strongly coming in, and my aim was to take it at the point where the distance between the two brush fences was about 12ft (3.6m a fairly short bounce). But even the best laid plans can go awry, and it was here that I had my fall with Michaelmas Day.

I am not really sure why it happened; it was just one of those unlucky things. Our approach to the fence was quite good and he jumped the first part well. He then jumped the second brush, and, as he touched down in the water, I thought we were in the clear. However, the next moment his back end disappeared from under him. He pitched to the right and I was shot out of the saddle. Nine times out of ten we would have jumped that fence without mishap, and possibly we would have survived a 'near miss', but it was not my lucky day.

I was wet through with the filthy water from the pond. I got back on and we jumped the next fence, but the horse was a bit hesitant – the

Fences 7 and 8
White Label Water
Garden

Vicarage Vee is not exactly the sort of fence you want to tackle straight after a fall – so I decided to retire him. With 60 penalties and a lot of big fences still left to jump, it did not seem worth carrying on. I preferred to save him for another day.

On Bahlua I rode the fence in exactly the same way as I had with Michaelmas Day. He jumped in well, and we had no problems.

The **Vicarage Vee** has never been a fence that I have liked. To jump the corner requires a great deal of accuracy and honesty from your horse. The alternative is over a horrible, wide ditch which the horses tend to jump very badly, so you have to take the ditch right beside the rail, where it is much narrower, and then turn away and come back at the rail. Although this takes a long time, I would choose this route on a green horse because the corner is a very big, testing fence. You are asking the horse to jump over a corner at an angle, with ditches lying in three directions. He therefore needs to have a lot of trust in his rider if he is to feel confident about jumping it where you ask him.

Fence 9
Vicarage Vee

As soon as I came out of the water at fence 8 on Bahlua, I made sure that I urged him forward again so that I could concentrate on my approach to the Vicarage Vee. I took him right out to the string on the left side of the track, and then looked out for two tall white posts that marked a gateway for people to cross the track. I knew that the second post was where I had to turn to get my line right into the Vicarage Vee. As I came along beside the string I woke up Bahlua with my legs, making sure that he was listening to me, and then turned and rode on my chosen line. I did not chase the horse but approached strongly, waiting to see the stride and holding him straight. I knew that once I came off that bend at the second post I would be on the right line, and I just kept my eye on the fence and kept coming to it. There was a little bit of leeway, and as Bahlua came into the corner he thought for a fraction of a second about going left, and I had to correct him instantly with the right rein. Then he jumped over it well.

Having just asked the horse to hold a very straight line at the Vicarage Vee, I thought it would be better to take what I thought was the least testing route at **The W**. This meant jumping the ditch first and then bouncing out over the point of an inverted V. The actual 'point' was slightly squared, and I think this helped the horses to back off a little and encouraged them to pick up their feet. You could safely push on as you came off the left-hand bend without worrying too much about accuracy, because the horse could not run out. Although a few people jumped one of the points of the W quite successfully, I felt that the alternative was kinder and did not take any longer.

Fence 10
The W

On to the **Coffin**. Big fences were coming up thick and fast now, and you had to think constantly about keeping your horse moving on between the obstacles. The approach to the Coffin was off a right-hand bend, but necessitated a slight swing to the left in order to arrive squarely at the fence. The obvious way to jump this one was straight through, because the alternative – jumping two parts of the T on each element – was very slow and involved a lot of pulling at the horse, which saps his energy. A steady, controlled approach was needed to the first rail, and then you had to ride strongly to get your horse down the bank, over the ditch and then one stride up the rise to the rail going out.

Bahlua tends to put his head up in the air when coming into a fence, and he did this as we came into the Coffin. I managed to keep him steady and he actually jumped in very well, but I think he ran down to the bottom of the coffin with his head in the air and didn't really see the ditch. He dropped a back leg into the ditch, which sat him down, and he couldn't

*Fence 11
Coffin*

recover his impetus quickly enough to jump the rail going out. For our second attempt at the final element we had to take the long route, and this ate up quite a few extra seconds.

So we now had 20 penalties. An unlucky stop at Badminton is a great disappointment, and I had to make up my mind quickly about whether to go on. If you decide to continue, you must be positive about it and go on as if nothing has happened; you cannot afford to pussy-foot around on a course like this. I decided I wanted Bahlua to finish the course, so I got him going again straight away, and tried to put the refusal completely out of my mind.

By now we had jumped four big, difficult fences in a row, so it was a relief to have a long, slightly uphill gallop to the lake. This gave us a chance to relax a little and I could let the horse gallop on without pushing him. I could not afford to let him switch off completely, though, because there was a very testing fence coming up at the lake. It helped to have the **Whitbread Drays** to jump on the way down to the water, as this woke the horse up a bit. This is a very upright fence, so you have to watch that you do not hit the front of it, but it usually rides well. I aimed for the tyre just left of the centre, to give the horse a good ground-line.

*Fence 12
Whitbread Drays*

At the **Lake** I had decided to take the bold route into the water. This meant jumping a curved rail with an option of going on the left, where there was a stride to the second rail, or on the right, where there were possibly two short strides. I went for the one stride because this would put us in line for the jump out of the lake, which came very quickly. I also felt that the two strides were going to be desperately short, and that might be a problem for a horse that was not very agile. The long option to the right of the curved rail was not that much easier, and its path led out into the lake, but if you had problems it would obviously be worth a try on the second attempt.

Fences 13, 14 and 15
The Lake

I took the first fence at the second panel of railings from the left, almost in the centre, aiming for the very centre of the second fence. This gave me one short stride. I had measured the distance as 7 yards (6.3m) at that point. A normal 'one stride' is 8 yards (7.2m) but for something like this I prefer to go for a short stride. The rails were very white and starey, and anyway a drop into water tends to make a horse back off a bit, so the shorter distance helps you to arrive at the fence in the right spot. If a horse stands off too far from a drop fence, he can sometimes be tempted to put down again. Coming in close gives him a bit more confidence, but then you have to hope that he will be neat in front. With the rails at the Lake fence it was necessary to ride strongly at the first element, in a strong show-jumping pace, to make sure that the horse jumped in well. Then, instead of a chasing stride, the horse needed a holding, pushing stride to make him jump into the water.

If you wanted to leave the lake by the short route you had to be very quick to find your line once you landed in the water; and you also had to break one of the classical cross-country principles of never jumping a drop fence at an angle. This was the only way to avoid heading off into deep water and overshooting the exit fence (something that happened to quite a few people). I tried to minimise the angle, and then started thinking about my line to the upturned boat as soon as I jumped the second set of rails. I knew that if we landed and took a stride off course it would be too late. It is very difficult to turn a horse in water, particularly in the lake at Badminton, where the water is quite deep.

You should never try to chase your horse through water if you can avoid

Bahlua jumping through the Lake. At this fence you had to break one of the classic cross-country rules of never jumping a drop fence on an angle – but it was the only way to avoid heading off into deep water and overshooting the fence out. The sequence shows that I had to slip my reins as we landed, to give the horse freedom of his head.

it. So once we landed in the lake I brought Bahlua in line for the exit fence and then sat quietly letting him go through the water, waiting to see what stride came out of it. As long as you keep a horse balanced through water and do not ask him to go too fast, he should cope well. If you panic and try to throw him off a long stride on to the bank you can end up in trouble. This is what happened to Ian Stark on Glenburnie. As they approached the bank Ian realised that they were too far away for three strides but too close for four, and they finished up by putting in a half stride so that Glenburnie paddled up the bank, and then he could not get himself together to jump the upturned boat.

My next time check (six minutes) was half-way up Worcester Avenue, but as I had already had a stop on Bahlua I was not particularly worried about time and I purposely did not check my watch. I let the horse gallop on. After our stop I didn't push him, but he still finished in 11 minutes 6 seconds (only 6 seconds over the optimum time) as he is a very quick horse. We obviously could have made the time if I had wanted to, which is good to know, but there was no point in chasing it.

Ian Stark with Glenburnie was not so lucky at the Lake. Ian got his stride wrong coming into the fence, and Glenburnie stumbled up the bank. Ian adopted the safety position, but there was nothing else he could do to help. Glenburnie landed on the bank in a muddle, and couldn't take off over the boat.

The **Worcester Rails**, fence 16, was a straightforward triple bar, but we came in a little close so I did not have a particularly nice ride over it. At a normal one-day event the Worcester Rails would have been regarded as a big fence, but at Badminton it served as something of a let-up. There was a slight drop on the landing side, and the ground then sloped away, so you had to sit up to avoid being pitched too far forward.

Next we rode down to the **Beaufort Staircase**. This was a new fence and we had to jink left slightly in our track to get straight for it. The options involved going straight up the middle of the steps and jumping a

Fence 16
Worcester Rails

narrow arrowhead, or going up the right-hand side of the steps and then turning sharp left, with two or three strides before jumping one of the wings of the arrowhead. The straight route looked difficult because there was only one, rather long, stride between the top of the third step and the arrowhead, so as you landed at the top of the staircase you would have to push your horse forward for the one stride, which would make it easier for him to run out.

Fence 17
Beaufort Staircase

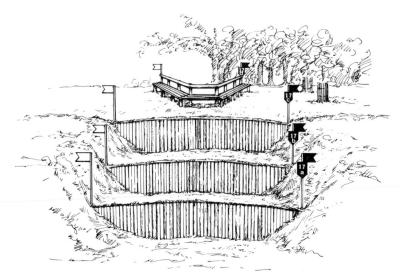

If you meet this type of steps correctly then they do not usually cause any trouble, but if you have problems at the first step you could arrive in a heap at the top, in which case taking the slightly longer alternative will be to your advantage, as it will give you more time to re-organise yourself. You need to approach this sort of fence quite steadily, otherwise the horse may jump on to the first step too flat, making it difficult for him to pick himself up and jump up the other steps. You have to think up, rather than forward, and even with very little speed a horse can manage to hop up quite easily. I felt it would be better to play safe at this fence and decided

Santi de la Rocha with Kinvarra taking the arrowhead straight on at the top of the Beaufort Staircase.

to go up the right-hand side of the staircase, land, take a stride and then turn sharp left and pop over the arm of the arrowhead. It did not take much longer than the direct route.

The Beaufort Staircase was followed by a gallop down to the **Snake**, a new fence. The most serious problem here was the approach. The ground in front of the fence was very unlevel so I had to drop Bahlua back to a fairly steady, balanced pace before we hit the rough ground so that it would be less likely to upset his stride. Having done that, I tried to ignore the ground and ride for the fence, attempting to keep Bahlua's mind on the obstacle ahead.

The direct route was not too difficult, but there was a big drop at the last element. The first two rails offered a bounce of about 13ft (3.9m) which was quite short. Then there was a stride to another rail with the ground sloping away as you took off, making a steep drop as you landed, and then you immediately met rising ground again. When I walked the course I thought that the last part would ride with a very big drop and that I would have to be prepared to sit up to help the horse back on his feet if

*Fences 18, 19 and
20
Snake*

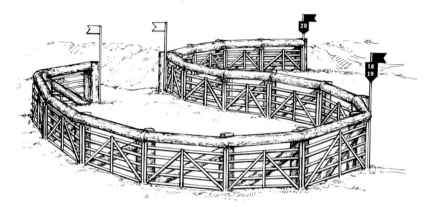

he pecked. I felt that it was the sort of fence on which a horse could easily catch his back legs and tip the rider forward out of the saddle.

I came in quite steadily on Bahlua and he popped into the bounce. Then I clucked at him and he jumped out well, not making too much of the drop. As long as you kept the forward momentum through the obstacle, the horse took care of the rest.

By this stage most of the horses were a bit weary of jumping drops so they were not leaping out over this one. In fact, this turned out to be a problem for Lorna Clarke. Fearliath Mor just did not go high enough and he scraped the last element with his belly and then shot Lorna out of the saddle. This can happen after a horse has tackled a lot of drops: he does not want to launch himself over another one because he knows there's going to be a big thump when he lands. There was nothing else Lorna could have done when coming into the fence; it was just one of those things.

The **Keeper's Bullfinch**, fence 21, always looks very big and formidable, but by this stage the horses show little concern about it. It is an attacking fence, and I felt confident about galloping down to it and riding it almost like a 'chase fence. It usually jumps very well.

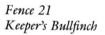

*Fence 21
Keeper's Bullfinch*

Vaughan Jeffries and Enterprise jumping the Keeper's Bullfinch. Vaughan was eliminated for riding the cross-country with his chin strap undone.

There followed a long gallop up to the **Quarry**. By now the horses were starting to feel a little tired and shell-shocked from jumping so many huge fences. Although you did not want to push your horse too hard on the gallop, it was important that when you reached the end of it you woke him up sharply, perhaps even with a slap of the stick, to focus his mind on the job in readiness for the Quarry.

There were three options at the quarry on this occasion, none of them being much easier or more time-consuming than the others, so it was a question of choosing the route that would best suit your horse. On the right there was a bank followed by a short stride to a very upright rail with

Fence 22
Quarry (first part)

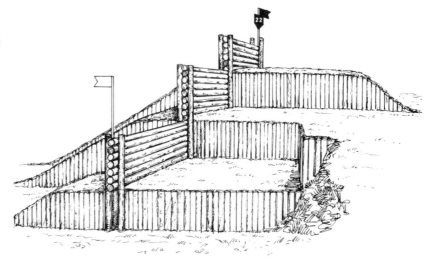

a big drop on the landing side. The middle part was approached on level ground, but this too had very upright rails that were even higher than the fence on the right, and it had a fairly big drop. On the left was a small step down and a bounce over another upright, with only a small drop into the quarry.

Lucinda Murray and Welton Fairgame negotiate one of the three options into the Quarry (fence 22). This was the route I chose because I thought it would suit Bahlua. It entailed popping down a bank and then bouncing out over the rails.

Fence 23
Quarry (second
part)

The right-hand route had looked the least appealing to me, but those who jumped it made it look easy. I decided to go for the left-hand route, as it seemed to be jumping fairly well, and the rail was quite low so the horse could see where the landing was. There was a very short distance in the bounce, and it looked a bit strange on the approach, so I brought Bahlua back to a trot to give him time to look at it. Then he popped down and just fiddled over it.

Once you have jumped the first part of the quarry, all you have to do is worry about your turn, which is usually quite tight, to the wall going out. This was a factor in choosing the option with the least drop, as it meant that I could have more control on landing. As soon as you are over the fence you have to look to the exit part of the quarry, turn and just wait for the stride. There is no need to chase your horse up the bank; they usually jump out of the quarry very well.

If you are behind the clock you can make up some time on the next stretch as you gallop on down to the **Trakehner** at **Huntsman's Close**, a wooded, shady section of the course. Bahlua was not tired at all at this stage. Being a full Thoroughbred he is a real galloping and jumping machine, and he was still pulling into his fences and jumping very well. He

Fence 24
Trakehner

was not under any pressure, and he never really got out of third gear, which is a lovely feeling. But the ground was firm, which made it easier.

The Trakehner always looks an imposing fence because of the huge ditch underneath it, but by this stage the horses are not really worried about that sort of thing. I simply forget about the ditch and just ride the log, but remembering that my horse may be getting tired, and it *is* a big fence. Even at this stage I like to keep my horse going, trying not to break the rhythm.

I took the Trakehner at a slight angle to give me a better line through the gate leading to the **Huntsman's Headache**. This latter was quite a technical and demanding fence to find at the end of a big course. The quickest route was on the left, over a big log, followed by a bounce up a bank and another bounce to a pair of rails. On the right you could put in one good stride before jumping up the bank, though the horse had to turn slightly to the left as he jumped. I decided that it would be easier at this stage for the horse to jump the longer alternative, and it did not take much more time.

Fence 25
Huntsman's
Headache

From there we rode on to the **Pheasant Feeder**, the only problem being to find our way through the trees of Huntsman's Close. The fence itself was straightforward. Then we galloped on to the **Lamb Creep**, which is a lovely fence. However, this is no time to relax and pat yourself on the

Fence 26
Pheasant Feeder

Fence 27
Lamb Creep

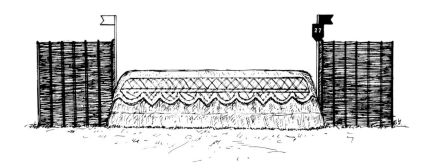

back; you will only trip over the last fences. I came down to the Lamb Creep quite strongly, but luckily Bahlua met it on a lovely stride and jumped it well. You would kick yourself, if you took many chances at this stage.

I always like to have a few seconds to spare to allow myself to take a pull at the last fence, the **Whitbread Bar**, which should be treated with respect. It is sited in the shadow of a solidly constructed building and has a black top rail that is quite difficult for the horses to see. After popping over that we then galloped on to the finish, and all that remained was for me to weigh-in.

Fence 28
Whitbread Bar

Bahlua soon recovered from his round. He was quickly checked for injuries, had his saddle removed and was walked back to the stables. By the time he arrived there he had stopped blowing, and it did not take long for him to cool down. I was pleased with our round. It was a pity about the slight mistake at the coffin, but I do not think there is anything either of us could have done about it.

Index

Page numbers in italics indicate illustrations